# Five Plays by Kishida Kunio

# Five Plays
## by
# Kishida Kunio

## EXPANDED EDITION

*Edited by*
David G. Goodman

*With translations by*
David G. Goodman
Richard McKinnon
J. Thomas Rimer
Kathleen Shigeta

East Asia Program
Cornell University
Ithaca, New York 14853

*The Cornell East Asia Series is published by the Cornell University East Asia Program and is not affiliated with Cornell University Press. We are a small, non-profit press, publishing reasonably priced books on a wide variety of topics relating to East Asia as a service to the academic community and the general public. We accept standing orders which may be cancelled at any time and which provide for automatic billing and shipping of each title in the series upon publication.*

*If after review by internal and external readers a manuscript is accepted for publication, it is published on the basis of camera-ready copy provided by the volume author. Each author is thus responsible for any necessary copy-editing and for manuscript formatting. Submission inquiries should be addressed to Editorial Board, East Asia Program, Cornell University, Ithaca, New York 14853-7601.*

# Contents

## PREFACE TO THE EXPANDED EDITION

Work on this book, which was originally published in 1989, began six years earlier, as I was preparing a course on modern Japanese drama for students at the University of Illinois at Urbana-Champaign. I found that there were few satisfactory English translations of representative works by modern Japanese playwrights available, and with the support of an Undergraduate Instructional Award from the University of Illinois, I began to translate *Land of Volcanic Ash* by Kubo Sakae and *The Two Daughters of Mr. Sawa* by Kishida Kunio. Subsequently, I contacted Professors Richard McKinnon and J. Thomas Rimer, who generously agreed to contribute translations to a collection of works by Kishida. The Center for East Asian and Pacific Studies at the University of Illinois provided a grant to facilitate the editing process.

The present volume reproduces the first edition, but it has been enhanced by a translation of Kishida's *Autumn in the Tyrols* by Kathleen Shigeta and myself. Certain errors and omissions in the first edition have also been corrected.

This volume is one in a series I have been preparing that presents English translations of works by modern Japanese dramatists. The other books in the series are *After Apocalypse: Four Japanese Plays of Hiroshima and Nagasaki* (Columbia University Press, 1986; Cornell East Asia Program, 1994); *Japanese Drama and Culture in the 1960s: The Return of the Gods* (M. E. Sharpe, 1988); and Kubo Sakae's *Land of Volcanic Ash* (Cornell East Asia Program, 1986).

As editor of the current volume, I have tried to achieve consistency in style, but I have otherwise made only minor changes in the translations. Each of the translators is responsible for the felicity and accuracy of his or her translation(s). I am responsible for the translation of *The Diary of Fallen Leaves*, which is a revised version of a translation prepared earlier by Professor Rimer, and for the translation of *Autumn in the Tyrols*, which is based on a translation by Ms. Shigeta.

vii

Finally, I would like to express my gratitude to Kishida Eriko, daughter of the playwright, for granting me permission to translate and publish her father's work.

David G. Goodman
January 1995

# INTRODUCTION

David G. Goodman

Thirty-five years after his death, Kishida Kunio remains a controversial figure. There is strong disagreement regarding the significance of his role in the history of *shingeki*, the Japanese modern theatre movement. Today, few would deny that Kishida was an important playwright, and young Japanese dramatists feel little compunction in accepting the Kishida Prize for Playwriting (*Kishida gikyoku shô*), Japan's major prize for new playwrights. But the consensus breaks down when Kishida's contribution to modern Japanese theatre is discussed.

There are basically three schools of thought about Kishida's legacy. The first, represented by American scholars like Donald Keene and J. Thomas Rimer, claims that Kishida "succeeded singlehandedly in creating a modern theater for Japan."[1] Rimer, whose *Toward a Modern Japanese Theatre: Kishida Kunio* is an indispensable guide to Kishida's work for English readers, proposes Kishida as the finest prewar Japanese playwright.[2]

The second school of thought, which predominates in Japan, argues that while Kishida may indeed have made innovations in playwriting technique, his role in the development of the shingeki movement was minimal. Kishida is regarded as the most outspoken proponent of the apolitical, "literary" school of playwriting, but his artistic accomplishments are viewed as having been overshadowed and to a large extent vitiated by his collaboration with Japanese militarism during the war.[3]

---

[1]Donald Keene, *Dawn to the West: Japanese Literature in the Modern Era--Poetry, Drama, Criticism* (New York: Holt, Rinehart and Winston, 1984), p. 477.

[2]J. Thomas Rimer, *Toward a Modern Japanese Theatre: Kishida Kunio* (Princeton: University Press, 1974), p. 56.

[3]This view is presented implicitly in most histories of the *shingeki* movement. See, for example, Sugai Yukio, *Shingeki no rekishi*, revised ed., Shin-Nihon shinsho 333 (Shin-Nihon shuppansha, 1984); and Shimomura Masao, *Shingeki*, Iwanami shinsho 256 (Iwanami shoten, 1956). The argument is set out explicitly in Ozaki Hirotsugu, *Chôran no hana ga saita yo* (Kage shobô, 1988), pp. 5-172.

The third and most recent school is represented by Watanabe Kazutami, whose 300-page revisionist biography of Kishida was published by the prestigious Iwanami Publishing Company in 1982.[4] Watanabe argues that Kishida's literary legacy has been unfairly obscured by the excessive attention paid to his wartime role. According to Watanabe, Kishida's involvement in the war was not collaboration but a form of resistance, and he argues that Kishida should be regarded as one who "sought to achieve real reform through the direct involvement of intellectuals in politics."[5]

Despite the extraordinary claims made for him by American scholars, only a handful of Kishida's plays have been translated into English. Those plays are not Kishida's best; the translations are uneven; and the texts have been difficult to obtain.[6] The present volume is therefore the first to bring together a representative sampling of Kishida's work in English. Written between 1925 and 1949, these plays span the entire course of Kishida's career. They include the plays critics have regarded as Kishida's best and that Kishida himself preferred.

My purpose in this introduction is to give my own assessment of Kishida's legacy and to make some sense out of the controversy surrounding him and his work. Needless to say, the opinions expressed here are my own and do not necessarily represent the views of my fellow translators.

**The Life**

Kishida was born on November 2, 1890, the eldest son in a family of eight children. His grandfather had been a ranking samurai in Kishū, present-day Wakayama prefecture, and his father, Kishida Shôzô, was an officer in an artillery unit of the Imperial Guard. As eldest son, Kishida

---

[4]Watanabe Kazutami, *Kishida Kunio-ron* (Iwanami shoten, 1982).

[5]Watanabe, p. 189.

[6]The plays are *Roof Garden*, in *The Passion by S. Mushakoji and Three Other Japanese Plays*, tr. Noboru Hidaka (Honolulu, 1933); *It Will Be Fine Tomorrow*, tr. Eiji Ukai and Eric Bell, *Eminent Authors of Contemporary Japan*, vol. 2 (Tokyo: Kaitakusha, 1931); and *Adoration*, the only play in this collection previously published, in *The Literary Review*, Autumn 1962. Recently, a translation of *The Swing* has also become available in J. Thomas Rimer, *Pilgrimages: Aspects of Japanese Literature and Culture* (Honolulu: University of Hawaii Press, 1988).

was expected to continue the family military tradition,[7] and he was duly educated in military schools. In 1912, he was commissioned as an officer in the Japanese Army. Kishida had little taste for the military life, however, and in 1914 he used a slight inflammation of the lungs as an excuse to resign his commission. Three years later, in 1917, he entered the French literature department of Tokyo University at the age of twenty-six. In 1919 he traveled to France, where he studied intensively for two years with Jacques Copeau, director of the Vieux Colombier company.

Kishida's father died in December 1922, and Kishida returned to Japan, arriving in July 1923. Although relations with his father had suffered severely because of his decision to abandon his military career, Kishida apparently felt compelled to return to Japan to assume his responsibilities as heir and head of the family.

Watanabe has written that, had it not been for his father's death, Kishida would have remained permanently in France;[8] and Kishida's conflicting loyalties to his family and his career, his military heritage and his dedication to literature, his love of France and his identity as a Japanese were to remain the basic tensions that characterized his life.

Kishida's return from France coincided with a major event in modern Japanese theatre history: the founding of the Tsukiji Little Theatre (*Tsukiji shôgekijô*). A catastrophic earthquake struck the Tokyo area on September 1, 1923, killing more than 100,000 people, destroying over 550,000 buildings, and leaving in excess of two million people homeless.[9] In order to facilitate reconstruction, the Tokyo city government relaxed construction codes, making it possible for the first time to build a theatre devoted solely to the production of modern plays. That theatre was the Tsukiji Little Theatre, which was built on the initiative of director Osanai Kaoru (1881-1928), with funds provided by Hijikata Yoshi (1898-1959), a devotee of modern drama who was also the scion of a wealthy, aristocratic family.

The announcement of plans to build a new theatre for modern plays was greeted enthusiastically by Japanese playwrights, who naturally assumed that it would be a showcase for their work. However, in a lecture delivered at Keio University on May 30, 1924, just two weeks before the

---

[7]Rimer, *Toward a Modern Japanese Theatre*, p. 57.

[8]Watanabe, p. 61.

[9]Janet E. Hunter, ed., *Concise Dictionary of Modern Japanese History* (Berkeley, CA: University of California Press, 1984), p. 86.

6 Goodman

Tsukiji was scheduled to open, Osanai declared that for a period of two years the Tsukiji would produce only translated European works. In effect, he slammed the door of the new theatre in the face of Japan's struggling modern playwrights, among them Kishida Kunio.[10]

Osanai's action precipitated a split in the nascent shingeki movement that has yet to heal completely. Kishida was alienated from Osanai for life by this incident, and he went on to become an outspoken leader of the anti-Tsukiji, "literary" stream of Japanese theatre.

In 1932, the first shingeki troupe to accept Kishida's aesthetic ideals was formed. It was the *Tsukijiza* (The Tsukiji Troupe), founded with Kishida's help by actor Tomoda Kyôsuke and actress Tamura Akiko. The same year, Kishida founded *Gekisaku* (Playwriting) magazine, which quickly became the main literary showcase for younger playwrights alienated from the left-wing mainstream of the modern theatre movement. Among the dramatists associated with the journal were Tanaka Chikao (b. 1905),[11] Uchimura Naoya (b. 1909), and Morimoto Kaoru (1912-1946). *Gekisaku* was so influential that this whole school of playwrights came to be known as the *Gekisaku-ha* or "*Playwriting* School."

With fellow playwrights Kubota Mantarô (1889-1963) and Iwata Toyoo (1893-1969), Kishida also founded *Bungakuza* (The Literary Theatre) in 1937. Because of its apolitical character and Kishida's powerful position within the government, The Literary Theatre was the only modern theatre troupe permitted to perform continuously through the war. It remains a major shingeki troupe today.

On August 19, 1940, the government arrested more than one hundred left-wing shingeki figures and ordered their troupes to disband. Virtually every prominent modern theatre figure was imprisoned, including Akîta Ujaku, Murayama Tomoyoshi, Kubo Sakae, Hisaita Eijirô, Takizawa

---

[10]For details on the Tsukiji Little Theatre, see Brian Powell, "Japan's First Modern Theatre--The Tsukiji Shôgekijô and Its Company, 1924-1926," *Monumenta Nipponica* (1975), 30(1):69-85; and John Allyn, Jr., "The Tsukiji Little Theatre and the Beginnings of Modern Theatre in Japan" (Ph.D. diss., University of California-Los Angeles, 1970).

[11]For an example of Tanaka's work, see Tanaka Chikao, *The Head of Mary*, in David G. Goodman, ed. and tr., *After Apocalypse: Four Japanese Plays of Hiroshima and Nagasaki* (New York: Columbia University Press, 1986), pp. 107-181. See also J. Thomas Rimer, "Four Plays by Tanaka Chikao," *Monumenta Nipponica* (Autumn 1976), 31(3).

Osamu, Matsumoto Kappei, Uno Jûkichi, Hosokawa Chikako, Hatta Motoo, Senda Koreya, and Okakura Shirô.[12]

Exactly two months later, on October 18, 1940, Kishida accepted the position of director of the cultural section of the newly organized *Taisei yokusankai* (Imperial Rule Assistance Association, IRAA), which replaced Japan's independent political parties and expedited the concentration of government power in the hands of the military. Kishida remained in this position for almost two years, until July 1942, a month after the IRAA was reorganized and lost its last vestiges of independence.

If Kishida was regarded as a traitor and collaborator by leaders of the shingeki movement in the postwar period, the least that can be said is that those feelings were not without foundation.

Watanabe describes Kishida's relationship with the war in the following terms.

It is true that Kishida Kunio supported the Pacific War just as he had supported the war with China. He also believed that Japan had to prevail. Furthermore, unlike his reaction to the beginning of the war with China [which had been lukewarm], Kishida responded with enthusiasm to the outbreak of war with the United States. Despite this fact, however, Kishida never compromised with the kind of xenophobia [*jôi no shisô*] that only emphasized Japan's uniqueness and disregarded universalism, that abandoned logical thought and viewed Japanese culture as absolute.[13]

Kishida continued to support the war even after he left the IRAA, however. As Ben-Ami Shillony has written,

The June 1943 issue of *Chûô kôron*, which announced the discontinuation of Tanizaki's novel [*The Makioka Sisters*], also carried the play *Kaeraji-to* (I Shall Not Return) by Kishida Kunio. Kishida, one of the founders of modern Japanese drama, was a known supporter of the war and until July 1942 had been the head of the Culture Department of the IRAA. In 1943 he published a book, *Chikara toshite [no] bunka* (Culture as Strength), in which he called on all

---

[12]Ozaki, p. 16.
[13]Watanabe, pp. 210-211.

writers to support the war. Nevertheless, the army authorities claimed that Kishida's play ridiculed the draft and they rebuked the *Chûô kôron* for publishing it.[14]

Donald Keene quotes a passage from *Chikara toshite no bunka* that must inevitably color any appraisal of Kishida Kunio:

It is our conviction that "Anglo-American" culture will be swept from our country and East Asia; indeed this is the object for which the war is being fought.... We must decisively reject the half-hearted attitude of openly saying that we have much to learn from America and England, or even of only thinking such things. We must be aware that this is not the issue at present. Fair-mindedness requires nothing of the kind, nor is this what is meant when one speaks of keeping calm and collected. If for some reason one absolutely must read an American or English book, it should be with feelings of hostility, putting to one's own use the contents of the books as if it were some item of war booty.[15]

Keene goes on to say that "Kishida insisted that the theater, the films, and other varieties of entertainment must all contribute to winning the war by serving (under government controls) to create the culture of Greater East Asia, in cooperation with other educational and propagandistic facilities."[16]

Kishida spent the end of the war in the mountains north of Tokyo. He published little until January 1, 1947, when he began serializing *Atena no nai tegami* (Letters to No One), which was sharply critical of the Japanese, whom Kishida called "freaks" (*kikei*).[17] On November 28,

---

[14]Ben-Ami Shillony, *Politics and Culture in Wartime Japan* (Oxford: Oxford University Press, 1981), pp. 124-125.

[15]Donald Keene, *Dawn to the West: Fiction* (New York: Holt, Rinehart and Winston, 1984), p. 936.

[16]Keene, *Dawn to the West: Fiction*, p. 936.

[17]*Atena no nai tegami*, including Kishida's controversial essay "Nihonjin kikeisetsu" (The Japanese as Freaks), was published in book form as *Nihonjin to wa nani ka* (What is a Japanese?) in June 1948. It was later reissued as *Nihonjin to wa--atena no nai tegami* (What is a Japanese: Letters to No One).

1947, Kishida was officially purged by the Occupation, both for his role in the IRAA and because he was a former army officer.[18]
After the war, Kishida was denounced as "a high-minded imperialistic humanist" (*kôketsu na teikokushugiteki yumanisto*) by left-wing intellectuals.[19] Even Kishida's sympathetic biographer Watanabe admits that when he read Kishida's work for the first time in 1948-49, he was unable to suppress the feeling that he was wrong to be impressed by the work of a wartime collaborator.[20]

Kishida published *Hayami onna-juku* (Hayami School for Girls), his first postwar play, in the July 1948 issue of *Chûô kôron*. With the exception of the propagandistic *Kaeraji to* (1943), it was Kishida's first play in twelve years. He wrote four other plays in the postwar period, which are generally regarded as satires on modern Japanese life.

Kishida collapsed on March 4, 1954, during the dress rehearsal for The Literary Theatre's production of Gorky's *Lower Depths*. He died at 6:32 A.M. the following day. He was sixty-three years old.

**The Plays**

Kishida wrote more than thirty plays between 1924 and 1930; and by 1935, that number had increased to fifty.[21] When the plays written after 1935 are included, Kishida's lifetime production comes to almost sixty scripts.

Critics have devised a number of schemes for periodizing Kishida's prolific output. The simplest and to my mind most useful is Abe Itaru's three-part division, which distinguishes between Kishida's early one-act plays or "sketches" (1924-1929), the multi-act works of his mid-career (1929-1936), and his postwar works.[22]

---

[18]Watanabe, pp. 242-243; 301n.
[19]This assessment was made by Chô Kôta, a poet and later an editor of the magazine *Teatro*. Chô was writing in the final issue of *Bungaku jihyô* in a column titled "bungaku kensatsu" ("literary prosecution") which was devoted to exposing the wartime responsibility of Japanese literary figures. Cited in Watanabe, p. 73.
[20]Watanabe, p. 303.
[21]Watanabe, p. 46.
[22]Abe Itaru, "Kishida Kunio-ron," in *Kindai geki bungaku no kenkyû* (Ōfûsha, 1980), pp. 7-51.

Abe believes that Kishida's early one-act plays are his most success-ful. He quotes Kishida's famous 1930 dictum that "One does not write a play in order 'to say something'; one 'says something' in order for there to be a play," as the dramatist's guiding principle in composing these works.[23] Most critics agree that Kishida's best plays are the ones com-posed with this principle in mind, plays written for their own sake and not to convey a message, particularly the short dramatic sketches Kishida wrote early in his career.[24] Two of the plays included in this collection--*Paper Balloon* (*Kami fûsen*, 1925) and *Cloudburst* (*Shûu*, 1926)--are charac-teristic of the dramatic sketches Kishida wrote during this period.

In the middle of his career, Kishida began to experiment with longer, multi-act works. Written in 1927, *A Diary of Fallen Leaves* (*Ochiba nikki*) is a transitional work, which basically expands the psychological realism of Kishida's earlier sketches into a longer format; while *The Two Daughters of Mr. Sawa* (*Sawa-shi no futari musume*, 1935) is a fully developed multi-act drama widely regarded as Kishida's best play. Kishida himself con-sidered *Two Daughters* his finest work,[25] and Rimer has called it "Kishida's most thoughtful and best-constructed play."[26] Abe believes, however, that these longer plays are generally less successful than the ear-lier works, because, initially at least, Kishida failed to realize that longer plays required more than a simple concatenation of psychological

---

In *Toward a Modern Japanese Theatre* Rimer divides Kishida's prewar career into four periods: 1925 to 1930, "when [Kishida] tried to search out the range of his artistic possibilities" (p. 154); 1930 to 1932, when "Kishida's work veered sharply back toward a representation of the [world as he found it and] the creation of specific social situations, treated with dry wit and a cold moralist's eye" (pp. 192-193); 1932 to 1936, a period "marked by a maturity in his observations of the quality of life in Japan . . . coupled with a similar maturity in writing technique, plus the happy occasion of writing with specific and talented players in mind" (pp. 211-212); and 1936 to 1939, when "the decay of social values . . . turned [Kishida] from reflective romantic drama to satire. . . .", p. 235.

[23] Abe, p. 25.

[24] See, for example, Saeki Ryûkô, "Kishida Kunio o yomu: *Sawa-shi no futari musume* o meguru hensô," in *Hôkô no shukusai: Shirai Kenzaburô koki kinen* (Asahi shuppan, 1986), p. 409 and passim; and Watanabe, p. 47.

[25] Rimer, *Toward a Modern Japanese Theatre*, p. 119.

[26] Rimer, *Toward a Modern Japanese Theatre*, p. 223. Other critics agree. See Abe, pp. 39-40; and Watanabe, pp. 114-116.

sketches.[27] Abe writes,

> Kishida Kunio perfected the dramatic style of writing he idealized, which would communicate "psychological rhythm," in his short, one-act plays, which he referred to as "plotless dramatic sketches." But he was never able to write in his multi-act "normal plays" [Kishida's term] the chaotic mixture of theme, form, and style that he conceived as an "orchestra of souls."[28]

When Kishida's longer plays did succeed, Abe believes it is because they are "plays written for their own sake" (*gikyoku no tame no gikyoku*) and not because of their content or message. They are, in his view, elaborations of Kishida's earlier plotless, contentless dramatic sketches.[29]

Abe regards Kishida's postwar plays as scarifying satires on Japanese society. *Adoration* (*Nyonin katsugô*, 1949), included here, is exceptional, having more in common with Kishida's prewar sketches.

Like Kishida's disciple Tanaka Chikao, however, Abe believes that Kishida died without ever making it clear what positive message he thought his theatre should convey. For Abe, therefore, Kishida's career was consistent from beginning to end; and his legacy resides in the plays written, not for their content or their message, but for themselves.[30]

Many critics have tried to read a message into Kishida's plays.[31] In fact, although the plays collected in this anthology were written over the course of a quarter-century, they share an eerie consistency. It is as if Kishida had been writing episodes in one long drama about a family that is slowly disintegrating but never completely dissolves.

Consider the plays in this anthology in chronological order. *Paper Balloon*, Kishida's most popular play,[32] concerns a young couple who have been married just one year. The newly-weds are having difficulty

[27] Abe, p. 36.
[28] Abe, pp. 36-37.
[29] Abe, p. 38.
[30] Abe, p. 50.
[31] See, for example, Nagahira Kazuo, *Kindai gikyoku no sekai*, UP sensho 93 (Tokyo daigaku shuppankai, 1972), pp. 139-161; and Ōzasa Yoshio, *Dorama no seishinshi* (Shinsuisha, 1983), pp. 193-222.
[32] Keene, *Dawn to the West*, p. 474.

communicating, and their marriage is already showing signs of strain.  In *Cloudburst*, a similar marriage dissolves before the honeymoon is over; and in *A Diary of Fallen Leaves*, the marriage has collapsed.  The wife has died, and the husband has left Japan, entrusting his daughter to the care of her grandmother.[33]

The theme of the absent or powerless father and the concomitant theme of the breakdown in patriarchal authority receives its fullest expression in *The Two Daughters of Mr. Sawa*.  Abroad for years, the father in *Two Daughters* is a widower who has neglected his family and is at least partially responsible for his wife's early demise.  He is incapable of projecting patriarchal authority, and relations in the family have suffered as a result.  During the course of the play, the intense mutual antipathy of Sawa's two daughters is revealed, as is his incapacity to do anything about it, and the atmosphere is reminiscent of Jean-Paul Sartre's *No Exit*, where hell is defined as "other people."

The inevitable consequences of this state of affairs are described in *Adoration*, where the emasculated father is found living with his daughter and procuring from a young prostitute the affection his daughter cannot or will not provide.

It is tempting to read Kishida's plays as thinly disguised autobiography.  Like the patriarchs in his plays, Kishida had spent time abroad; and also like them he was the father of daughters.  But the resemblance ends there, for Kishida's marriage was a happy one, and his relations with his daughters were good.[34]

Japanese ideology in the prewar period stressed the notion of Japan as an extended family under the patriarchal authority of the emperor.  The family that slowly disintegrates in Kishida's work might therefore be understood as a synecdoche for Japan as a whole.  Kishida might have been attempting to explore the dynamics of the Japanese spirit in a period of rapid and disorienting social change, exacerbated by the encounter with Western culture.  He might have been describing the foibles of people in what he perceived to be a period of spiritual and moral decline.  In fact, this is probably the most common reading of Kishida's work today.

While this metaphorical reading of Kishida's work has its attractions, however, it is ultimately unsatisfying.  As Abe points out, Kishida's plays are far too small-scale to successfully capture the powerful forces and the wrenching conflicts that have characterized Japanese life in modern times;[35] and Saeki notes that Kishida frequently and vociferously objected to theme-centered drama in his theoretical articles.[36]  As Mishima Yukio put it, Kishida's plays are chamber music for the theatre, and they fail completely to capture the orchestral grandeur of modern Japanese history.[37]

**Kishida and Kubo**

The fact that Kishida's plays cannot be taken seriously as social commentary becomes starkly apparent when they are compared to the work of Kubo Sakae (1900-1958), who was heir to Osanai Kaoru's legacy and the most important playwright in the shingeki mainstream during the 1930s.

Even a cursory comparison of Kishida's work with Kubo's most important play, *Land of Volcanic Ash*, reveals the difference between the two dramatists.[38] Kishida's works are brief and evocative. Kubo's play, by contrast, is monumental, running to hundreds of pages, with dozens of characters, and encompassing the whole of social reality. Kishida's plays are invariably set in a narrowly defined space--a closed room, a garden, a patio--and have an almost claustrophobic atmosphere; Kubo's horizons are as broad and open as those of Hokkaido, where he was born and which he described in *Land of Volcanic Ash*.[39]

While both Kubo and Kishida were trying to devise a "realistic" dramaturgy, their definition of "realism" and "reality" was radically at odds. Reality for Kishida was essentially a psychological state to be described, or rather suggested, through imagistic, poetic language. As he wrote in 1935, "I believe we can say that the essential nature of the theatre lies in a progressive rhythm of images that gives a heightened sense of life through the medium of the stage."[40] For Kubo, by contrast, reality was above all a social phenomenon best understood with the tools of objective social science. Also writing in 1935, he described realism in the following

---

[33]Kishida also wrote a novel with the title *A Diary of Fallen Leaves* (*Ochiba nikki*). It was serialized in *Fujin kôron* from June 1936 to May 1937. The novel is not identical to the play, but picks the story up where the play leaves off, with the return to Japan of the son and the death of his mother.

[34]See Rimer, *Toward a Modern Japanese Theatre*, p. 284-286.

[35]Abe, p. 44.

[36]Saeki, p. 409.

[37]Quoted in Abe, p. 51.

[38]Kubo Sakae, *Land of Volcanic Ash*, tr. David G. Goodman, East Asian Papers 40 (Ithaca, NY: Cornell China-Japan Program, 1986).

[39]For a discussion of the special place of Hokkaido in modern Japanese literature, see Paul Anderer, *Other Worlds: Arishima Takeo and the Bounds of Modern Japanese Fiction* (New York: Columbia University press, 1984), pp. 19-40.

[40]Quoted in Rimer, *Toward a Modern Japanese Theatre*, pp. 138-139.

manner:

> Our realism captures the innermost truths of man and society and, cutting through all facades, shows how--while antagonistic, contradictory, and interacting in complex ways--they develop toward a higher stage of unity. Without reducing them to stereotypes and without vulgarization, we clarify them in terms of the typical form of [class] conflict and formulate them with artistry and style.[41]

Written as a manifesto for the newly formed *Shinkyô* (New Cooperative) troupe, Kubo's statement emphasizes man in society. "Reality" and "truth" are intimately related to a complicated series of interacting phenomena, including, but not restricted to, individual psychology.

By contrast, Kishida's realism emphasized individual psychology almost to the exclusion of social phenomenon. He described his ideal in the manifesto he drafted with Kubota Mantarô and Iwata Toyoo when they founded The Literary Theatre:

> Avoiding makeshifts, pedantry, or subservience to politics, we would like to offer to the intelligent general public through the medium of the stage a glimpse of a genuine "entertainment for the soul." We wish to avoid both the vague "theatrical" atmosphere that has been part of the drama in Japan until now, as well as the various crude aspects of the radical elements in the New Theatre movement. We wish to create a theatre with an intimate connection with the emotional realities of contemporary life.[42]

In short, while Kishida's plays do portray the kind of steady degeneration in the Japanese family that I described above, it would be a mistake to regard them as an extended metaphorical commentary on the changes taking place in Japanese society. As Abe Itaru has noted, Kishida was simply not interested in exploring the historical sources or social implications of this phenomenon.[43] Rather, he was concerned with what he called "the emotional realities of contemporary life."

---

[41] Quoted in Sugai Yukio, *Nihon kindai engeki ronsô-shi* (Miraisha, 1979), pp. 210-211.

[42] Rimer, *Toward a Modern Japanese Theatre*, pp. 118-119.

[43] Abe, pp. 43-44.

## Kishida's "Emotional Reality"

For Kishida Kunio, what was the emotional reality of contemporary life? Fukuda Tsuneari, one of Kishida's most prominent disciples, has identified an overwhelming sense of disintegration (*hôkai*) as the most salient characteristic of that reality. He describes Kishida as a man who struggled valiantly to deal with his sense of disintegration but who was essentially paralyzed, trapped between conflicting desires to flee from it and to exacerbate the process in order to get it over with quickly. Fukuda notes that Kishida's plays lack the basic dramatic development one might expect in them, from a state of equilibrium to a state of disintegration, and he accounts for this deficiency by saying that Kishida anticipated disintegration and tried to preempt it in his work. According to Fukuda, this is why, in plays like *The Two Daughters of Mr. Sawa* and *Adoration*, the family has already disintegrated beyond repair before the curtain even rises.[44]

A sense of paralysis and dislocation are two other characteristics of the emotional reality Kishida describes in his work. Beginning with *Paper Balloon*, where the young couple are trapped in their bungalow, unable to decide how to spend their free time, Kishida's plays are almost without exception documents of immobility and paralysis. No one ever escapes in Kishida's plays. At the same time, populated by deracinated cosmopolitans like Sawa Kazuhisa, his plays frequently describe human dislocation in both time and space. As Ōzasa Yoshio has commented, the consistent psychic reality throughout Kishida's work is dislocation (*sogokan*), a sense of "being alone in the world without any reality with which to affiliate oneself."[45]

In short, Kishida's plays are dramas that consistently evoke what Robert Jay Lifton has called the psychic equivalents of death: "image-feelings of separation, disintegration, and stasis."[46] Put another way, death

---

[44]Fukuda Tsuneari, "Kishida Kunio-ron," *Watakushi no engeki kyôshitsu* (Shinchôsha, 1961), pp. 286-298.

[45]Ōzasa, p. 201.

[46]Lifton develops his concept of death equivalents and their role in human psychological development most completely in *The Broken Connection: On Death and the Continuity of Life* (New York: Simon and Schuster, 1979), where he writes, for example, "Images of death begin to form at birth and

16  Goodman

expressed in terms of disintegration, paralysis (stasis), and dislocation (separation) was the emotional reality that Kishida evoked in his work. Fukuda Tsuneari does not explicitly define what he means by "disintegration" as the central reality in Kishida's emotional life, but the clear implication is that it was traditional Japanese culture in the modern period, particularly the culture of the military elite of which Kishida was a part. Kishida was intensely ambivalent toward the military. By resigning his commission and going to France to study literature, he had not only rejected a career in the army but also disobeyed his father and betrayed his family heritage. Nevertheless, Fukuda describes Kishida's personal moral code as a form of *bushidô* or "warrior ethics," and he defines Kishida's basic personality as a manifestation of "the Japanese martial spirit."[47] Ozaki also postulates that Kishida's willingness to participate in Japan's wartime military government and his acceptability to that government was attributable in part to his military background and to his personal friendships with the military officers with whom he had been trained.[48]

In other words, Kishida's perception of the disintegration of traditional Japanese culture; his ambivalence toward that process of disintegration; his conflicted sense of paralysis, that is, of being unable to do anything about it; and the resulting sense of dislocation he experienced, which he frequently expressed in his plays in the form of Japanese cosmopolitans caught between Western and Japanese culture and comfortable in neither, were rooted in, reinforced and exacerbated by his personal sense of guilt over having opposed his father's demand that he pursue a military career and his sense of having betrayed his family's samurai heritage.

---

continue to exist throughout the life cycle. Much of that imagery consists of 'death equivalents'--image-feelings of separation, disintegration, and stasis. These death equivalents evolve from the first moment of life, and serve as psychic precursors and models for later feelings about actual death. Images of separation, disintegration, and stasis both anticipate actual death imagery and continue to blend and interact with that imagery after its appearance." (p. 53)

For other case studies of modern Japanese intellectuals that employ Lifton's method, see Robert Jay Lifton, Shûichi Katô, and Michael R. Reich, *Six Lives, Six Deaths: Portraits from Modern Japan* (New Haven: Yale University Press, 1979).

[47]Fukuda, pp. 288-289.
[48]Ozaki, pp. 31-33.

**The Ahistorical Nature of Kishida's Plays**

Kishida's sense of disintegration, paralysis, and dislocation manifested itself in his plays in a variety of ways, but most importantly in a pronounced antipathy toward history. Kishida's characters are hardly representative of the Japanese of their day. With the exception of Namiki in *The Roof Garden* (*Okujô teien*, 1926), all of his major characters are at least middle-class and frequently members of a tiny elite. They have typically spent time abroad and speak foreign languages fluently; the women walk away from their husbands, work in record companies, and marry foreigners; and even Kishida's most ordinary characters, like the young couple in *Paper Balloon*, are part of an upwardly mobile, urban elite, who live in fashionable bungalows in "an elegant and beautiful residential area" of Tokyo described by a visiting American businessman as "a Los Angeles in miniature."

As Saeki has pointed out, however, Kishida had no sociological interest in the bourgeoisie as such. Rather, he used bourgeois characters and the "rootless cosmopolitans" who appear in his plays as vehicles to express the experience of meaninglessness, of anomie, of discontinuity in the modern world.[49] For these characters, history does not exist. Instead of history, their lives are grounded in the rituals of daily life. The way Sawa prepares coffee in the final act of *Two Daughters* is a good example of such a ritual. Almost without exception, their lives are devoid of any larger significance. Disintegrating and divorced from the continuum of history, the most prominent emotion Kishida's characters experience is not despair but boredom.

Referring to *The Two Daughters of Mr. Sawa*, Saeki explains the significance of this characteristic of Kishida's dramaturgy.

In short, we are denied by the play itself the possibility of piecing together a story or a drama behind the events that take place on stage. Everything that happens just happens; the conflict is unclear; the past does not explain the present; and in that present there are only characters, each facing in his or her own direction and saying whatever comes into his or her head; time is for the most part motion-

---

[49]Saeki, p. 433.

less, inorganic time--and in a realm where the connection between past and present, where the process of cause and effect does not exist, morality does not exist either. In a word, all that we have here is the present, a minute differentiation of moments within a motionless expanse of time, and word games. . . . There is loss. But that loss is the loss of time, the lack of a theme, the absence of a story.

What Kishida Kunio introduced into Japanese modern theatre in the 1920s was this sense of time, a sense of time that, from the point of view of the shingeki mainstream represented by the Tsukiji Little Theatre, was at least idiosyncratic and, more to the point, obstructionist, wherein the phenomenon of time is manifested solely in the here-and-now, where there is no history, and where all that exists is language. . . .[50]

In fact, Kishida expressed the bourgeois loss of history as a quality of language. "More than anything," Saeki writes, "I believe Kishida wanted to express the loss of correspondence between words and things (that is, their reality)."[51]

Not history but daily life; not dramatic conflict but the theme of absence; plots that, while constantly flirting with reality, are devoid of both reality and life; tales of impotence--what Kishida depicted was the fate of contemporary language, which exists only as a metaphenomenon, and the life of the bourgeoisie was the perfect vehicle for it.[52]

## Kishida, Jacques Copeau, and the Poetic Theatre

Because of his antipathy toward history and his emphasis on language as the heart and soul of the theatre, Kishida is widely regarded as a "literary" playwright. In fact, as Donald Keene has noted, "His best plays were rarely performed, and have enjoyed only sporadic revivals even in recent days. . . . But inasmuch as Kishida insisted on the literary aspects of the theater, it was not an unmitigated disaster that his plays have tended

---

[50]Saeki, p. 410.
[51]Saeki, p. 432.
[52]Saeki, p. 433.

to be read rather than seen."[53]

Kishida's literary approach to the theatre was not original but was learned from French director Jacques Copeau, with whom Kishida had studied in Paris in 1921 and 1922.

Copeau's Vieux Colombier company enjoyed its greatest success in 1921 and 1922. In fact, writes Maurice Kurtz, "This two year period found the Vieux-Colombier's name repeated throughout the world as a mecca for theatrical art."[54]

Kishida's relationship with Copeau differed significantly from the relationship of other Japanese theatre figures with their European models: Osanai Kaoru with Stanislavsky, Hijikata Yoshi with Meyerhold, and Iwata Toyoo with Pirandello. In the case of other shingeki figures, the relationship was one of inspiration; but in Kishida's case, Saeki argues, Copeau provided an absolute paradigm.[55] Fukuda has also commented on the parochialism of Kishida's tastes, noting that Kishida displayed little enthusiasm for classical playwrights like Shakespeare or Racine but was totally devoted to modern French drama.[56]

Saeki argues convincingly that Kishida copied Copeau's approach to the theatre in virtually every respect.[57] Kishida's distaste for kabuki and his insistence on the importance of actor training, for example, were a Japanese version of Copeau's distaste for the style of melodramatic acting that had been practiced in France since the nineteenth century and Copeau's desire to train "intellectual" actors. Kishida's critique of the emphasis on theatricalism and of the cult of the director in the Tsukiji Little Theatre was a reiteration of Copeau's critique of directors like Max Reinhardt, Gordon

---

[53]Keene, *Dawn to the West: Japanese Literature in the Modern Era--Poetry, Drama, Criticism*, pp. 477-478.

Actually, Kishida's plays are being performed more regularly today than at perhaps any other time. Two groups in particular have made long-term commitments to producing Kishida's work, one led by freelance director Sueki Toshifumi and the other, the Tokyo Engeki Ensemble, led by director Hirowatari Tsunetoshi.

[54]Maurice Kurtz, "Biography of a Theatre: Jacques Copeau's Vieux-Colombier" (Ph.D. diss., Columbia University, 1946), p. 177.

[55]Saeki, p. 412.

[56]Fukuda, p. 288.

[57]Saeki, pp. 411-418. Watanabe agrees with this assessment. See Watanabe, pp. 29-31.

Craig, and Stanislavsky.  But above all, Kishida's insistence on poetic language as the heart of the theatre was quintessential Copeau.[58]

Kurtz has written that Copeau's "dream was a non-theatrical theatre, one from which he would strike the word 'theatre' with all its artifice, awkwardness, compromise and dishonesty";[59] and as early as 1913, when he founded the Vieux Colombier, Copeau wrote, "We must not confuse scenic conventions with dramatic conventions ... for the new drama let us have a bare stage!..."[60] He sought an absolutely pure theatre and the "complete elimination of all stage devices which monopolized an audience's attention."[61]

On Copeau's bare stage, poetic language would rule.  "The poet alone is the real origin and life of all drama," he wrote.[62]  The actor, by contrast, was to be essentially transparent:

> The Vieux-Colombier actor was never permitted to reproduce reality. He suggested it.  This was a sharp break from the manner of an Antoine or a Stanislavsky who placed all emphasis on the actor's ability to convey the physical and mental counterpart of his characterization.  Yet what Copeau took from them, whose realistic staging he considered basically false and inartistic, was their actor's sincerity and naturalness.  These were used by him to attain an objective view of the character played rather than the actual character, as subjectively reproduced by a Stanislavsky.  *Copeau sought to convey the image of reality where most schools of acting believed in the reality of the image.*
>
> Essentially, Copeau's mise on scène was "the actor in movement on a surface."  A Vieux-Colombier production was one rhythmic whole which had the effect of a visual symphony on its spectators. . . . Tragedy was also staged with rhythm, with an interior psychological rhythm.[63]

Kishida espoused precisely the same philosophy.  One of his major

---

[58]Saeki, p. 412.
[59]Kurtz, p. 116.
[60]Quoted in Kurtz, p. 24.
[61]Kurtz, p. 152.
[62]Quoted in Kurtz, p. 153.
[63]Kurtz, pp. 151-152.  Italics added.

collections of theatre essays is titled *Hadaka no butai* (The Naked Stage). "Ideas," he wrote, "are always backed by emotions; and those emotions always flow according to a psychological rhythm."[64] For Kishida, "Beauty" in a work of drama "exists in the fascination of 'the spoken word' in every sense, that is, in the spoken word as the most direct and at the same time the most suggestive expression of human life, the spoken word as 'the most rhythmic sound (movement) of the human soul.'"[65] The musical metaphor continues: "A character is composed when the inner workings of the mind combine with interesting character traits. Themes develop from the ordering and relationship of characters thus composed, and 'an orchestra of souls' results."[66]

What is interesting in these theoretical pronouncements is not only the close resemblance between Kishida's philosophy of the theatre and Copeau's, but the musical imagery both men favored, for music is the most self-referential of the arts. Both Copeau and Kishida, in true symbolist fashion, aimed at a language that would refer only inward, that would reflect and convey the palpitations of the individual heart, but that would convey no message and have as little relation with the outside world as possible.

In Copeau's case, however, there was a religious vision underlying his image of the theatre. Kurtz writes, for example, that

On January 14 [1920], a modern *mystère* by Ghéon on the life of Saint Alexis, *Le Pauvre sous l'escalier*, received its first performance midst great applause from the first-night audience. . . . For Copeau it was another experiment, this time to discover how close the theatre could be brought to the church, whether people would attend the theatre as they do a religious rite and then leave with the same exaltation and reverence as from a house of worship."[67]

A year earlier, Copeau had explicitly acknowledged his aim of recapturing the religious character of the theatre, of realizing theatre as religious ritual.[68] But in fact, Copeau's religious vision went back even farther, to

---

[64]"Butai no kotoba," quoted in Abe, p. 23.

[65]"Engeki no honshitsu," quoted in Abe, pp. 30-31.

[66]"Engeki no honshitsu," quoted in Abe, p. 31.

[67]Kurtz, p. 136.

[68]Copeau, *Registres I: Appels* (Paris: Gallimard, 1974), p. 133. Quoted in

his initial conception of the theatre.  In letters he wrote to the actor Louis
Jouvet in 1915 and 1916, for example, he described the theatre in language
that was consistently religious and profoundly Roman Catholic.  He
understood the theatre as a religious vocation, a holy enterprise;  and he
described the successful actor as being in a state of grace.  As he wrote on
August 25, 1915,

> Yes, absolute communion, communion of the heart and one's whole
> being for a work as thrilling, as important, as holy as that of the
> artisans of the middle ages (and like them, with simplicity, without
> pretension....)[69]

This medieval community engaged in a work of holiness was
Copeau's ideal.  But in the end, Jouvet and Copeau's other coworkers
could not share his religious vision.  Jouvet, Jules Romains, Georges
Duhamel, and others left the Vieux Colombier in 1922, impatient with
Copeau's asceticism and his refusal to capitalize on the company's success.
The result was that 75% of the theatre's subscribers did not renew their
subscriptions for the following season.[70]  Copeau refused to compromise,
and the next season (1923-24) was the theatre's last.  On May 3, 1924,
Copeau announced that the Vieux Colombier would close its doors forever.

After the Vieux Colombier closed, Copeau moved to Burgundy to
work among the peasantry in the spirit of medieval communion he had
sought to realize in the company, and in 1925 he formally converted to
Catholicism.  However, "this rediscovered faith envelopped [sic] him completely and made him almost unapproachable to his pupils."[71]   And
according to André Gide, writing in 1931, Copeau "shun[ned] admitting to
himself that between Catholicism and dramatic art there could be no
alliance."[72]

Kishida probably understood the religious basis of his mentor's
vision.  The references to Anatole France's work in *A Diary of Fallen
Leaves* suggests that Kishida may even have flirted with Catholicism himself.  In particular, the musical reference to *Thaïs*, which concerns the con-

---

Saeki, p. 417.
[69]Quoted in Kurtz, pp. 62-63.
[70]Kurtz, p. 189.
[71]Kurtz, p. 222.
[72]Quoted in Kurtz, p. 234.

version to Christianity of an Alexandrian courtesan who believes her life has been wasted, suggests that Kishida appreciated Christianity's promise of redemption.[73] It is also worth noting that Kishida's two principal disciples, Fukuda Tsuneari and Tanaka Chikao, have both espoused Christianity.[74] But as Fukuda notes, for Kishida himself, Christian faith was not a viable option.[75]

What is left, then, is the void. One of the notable things about Kishida's characters is that they are futureless. From the young couples in *Paper Balloon* and *Cloudburst* to the Dowager in *A Diary of Fallen Leaves*, Sawa in *The Two Daughters of Mr. Sawa*, and the old man in *Adoration*, the major characters in Kishida's best plays live, staring into the abyss. Estranged from the past, they have no hope for the future.

To be sure, Kishida's plays are entertaining, on occasion even funny. But the humor in Kishida's plays is a function of their nihilism. Kishida understood the relationship between the humor in his plays and the emptiness his characters experience. As he wrote after the war, "I believe that 'comedy' is above all the product of a profound sense of sadness with regard to humanity and history."[76] It is entertaining to watch Kishida's characters while away the time; but, as Tsuno Kaitarô has observed, from Chekhov to Beckett, the unique pleasure of modern drama is to watch the ingenious ways people find to kill time.[77] In this sense, Kishida is a typically modern playwright.

**Kishida's Legacy**

In 1931, Kishida wrote, "I have long believed that in the entire history of world theatre, the greatest and most noble monuments are the plays

---

[73]See the synopsis of *Thaïs* in the notes to *A Diary of Fallen Leaves* below.

[74]See Tanaka's *The Head of Mary* and my discussion of his work in *After Apocalypse*, pp. 105-181. Regarding Fukuda, see Benito Ortolani, "Fukuda Tsuneari: Modernization and Shingeki," in Donald H. Shively, ed., *Tradition and Modernization in Japanese Culture* (Princeton: Princeton University Press, 1971), p. 474 and *passim*; and Fukuda Tsuneari and Takeuchi Yoshimi, "Gendaiteki jôkyô to chishikijin no sekinin" *Tenbô,* September 1965, p. 25.

[75]Fukuda, p. 288.

[76]Quoted in Abe, p. 49.

[77]Tsuno Kaitarô, *Mon no mukô no gekijô* (Hakusuisha, 1972), pp. 9-25 and *passim*.

of Chekhov and *nô* drama."[78] Kishida's feeling of affinity for Chekhov is understandable. Kwok-Kan Tam has written, for example, that *The Two Daughters of Mr. Sawa* displays "the indirect action of Anton Chekhov," and that "Sawa has the image of the superfluous character portrayed in Chekhov's drama."[79] But the reference to nô is unexpected and intriguing. Kishida admits that he has seen few nô plays, but he praises them, especially the most impenetrable (*mottomo imi no tsûjinai kyoku*), as being close to his ideal of "pure theatre." Unencumbered by meaning and highly imagistic, they present "the magic of words translated into acting on the stage." And he concludes, "It is precisely in the disconnected linguistic images that transcendent life flows, and it is there that one finds the joy of feeling a 'truth' that is not of this world."[80]

Judging from these comments, Kishida seems to have hoped that his plays, like nô drama, would communicate through imagistic language a transcendent reality and a supernatural truth.[81] Perhaps he also hoped to emulate "the moral purpose behind Chekhov's imitation of reality."[82] But even Kishida's most ardent defenders are reluctant to conclude that he succeeded in achieving these goals. As Tanaka Chikao suggested in the comment already cited, Kishida died without ever making it clear what he was trying to affirm in his plays;[83] and Fukuda Tsuneari, while praising Kishida for having created a fresh, new kind of psychological drama, concludes that in the final analysis its meaning is ambiguous and that it has been left to him and the other heirs to Kishida's legacy "to make visible the invisible drama of Kishida's work."[84]

---

[78]"Gekidan sayu tenbô," quoted in Abe, pp. 32-33. For Kishida's complete comment, see his *Gendai engekiron*, revised ed. (Hakusuisha, 1936, 1950), pp. 142-143.

[79]Kwok-Kan Tam, "Love as Redemption in Kishida Kunio's Domestic Tragedy," *Asian Culture Quarterly* (Spring 1986), XIV(1):1;4.

[80]*Gendai engekiron*, p. 143.

[81]The transcendent reality and supernatural truth of nô is essentially that of Buddhism. See William R. LaFleur, "Zeami's Buddhism: Cosmology and Dialectic in Nô Drama," *The Karma of Words: Buddhism and the Literary Arts in Medieval Japan* (Berkeley, CA: University of California Press, 1983), pp. 116-132.

[82]Robert Brustein, "Foreword," to Ann Dunnigan, tr., *Chekhov: The Major Plays* (New York: New American Library, 1964), p. viii.

[83]See Abe, p. 50.

[84]Fukuda, pp. 290; 298.

In the end, it is this opaque quality of Kishida's work, its ultimate ambiguity, its lack of a comprehensible moral cosmology beyond what Fukuda calls the playwright's personal "rigorism"[85] that is its most outstanding characteristic and its greatest weakness. These same qualities may be held responsible for Kishida's wartime collaboration and for the ambivalence postwar generations have felt toward him. Essentially nihilistic as it was, Kishida's dramaturgy provided no principles, no rationale for resisting the war. Staunchly ahistorical and divorced from social reality, it provided no barricade against barbarism.

After his death in 1954, Kishida's legacy has been taken up by two different kinds of dramatists. Kishida's disciples Tanaka Chikao and Fukuda Tsuneari have sought to supply the missing element in Kishida's dramaturgy. As I have already noted, both profess Christianity. The fact is significant, because what Tanaka and Fukuda have done in effect is to try to supply the missing element in Kishida's drama, the moral dimension that would have made it truly comparable to the work of Copeau, Chekhov, and the nô. They identified, in a way that was valid for themselves, although not necessarily for Kishida, the transcendent reality and supernatural truth that Kishida aspired to communicate. Tanaka's *The Head of Mary* is a good example of a work of psychological realism and linguistic innovation composed under Kishida's influence but informed by a Roman Catholic theology.[86]

The other heir to Kishida's legacy is Betsuyaku Minoru (b. 1937). Far from being a disciple of Kishida, Betsuyaku emerged from the cultural tumult surrounding the opposition to renewal of the U.S.-Japan Mutual Security Treaty in 1960. He is part of what I have called the post-shingeki movement.[87] However, Betsuyaku shares Kishida's emphasis on a naked stage and the primacy of language, and he can therefore be seen as the post-shingeki playwright who most closely resembles the older dramatist.

In essence, Betsuyaku has adopted a strategy opposite to the one chosen by Tanaka and Fukuda. Rather than fill in the void that lies beneath the surface of Kishida's work, Betsuyaku affirms it, examines it, and makes it the centerpiece of his drama. Beginning with plays like *The*

---

[85]Fukuda, pp. 288-290. Fukuda uses the English term.

[86]See my translation in *After Apocalypse*, pp. 115-181.

[87]For a discussion of the "post-shingeki movement" see David G. Goodman, *Japanese Drama and Culture in the 1960s: The Return of the Gods* (Armonk, NY: M. E. Sharpe, 1988).

*Elephant*, which deals with survivors of Hiroshima, Betsuyaku uses a precise, elliptical language reminiscent of Kishida's idiom and relates it to the historical reality of the nuclear age. Like Samuel Beckett and the other Absurdist playwrights who have influenced him, Betsuyaku seeks to expose the human condition in the radically futureless nuclear age.[88]

## Conclusion

The plays of Kishida Kunio are a form of psychological realism. They are a projection of the playwright's personal emotional reality onto the stage. Kishida's emotional reality was dominated by his inability to resolve the central dilemma in his life, the conflict with his father over his obligations to state and family.

Kishida's inability to resolve this central dilemma gave rise to the basic tensions in his emotional life. For example, having refused to fulfill his family obligations as eldest son, Kishida left Japan, only to return in order to fulfill precisely those same obligations. Despite his distaste for the military, he became the only major modern theatre figure to collaborate more or less unconditionally with Japanese militarism. Furthermore, despite his devotion to France and French literature and his alienation from the Japanese, whom he called "freaks," he became an outspoken and influential xenophobe during the war.

Kishida experienced the inability to resolve these tensions in his personal emotional life as feelings of paralysis, disintegration, and dislocation.

---

[88] For translations of Betsuyaku's work, see *The Move* in Ted T. Takaya, ed. and tr., *Modern Japanese Drama* (New York: Columbia University Press, 1979), pp. 203-272; and *The Elephant* in David G. Goodman, ed. and tr., *After Apocalypse: Four Japanese Plays of Hiroshima and Nagasaki* (New York: Columbia University Press, 1986), pp. 185-248.

See also, Robert Rolf's informative articles, "Betsuyaku Minoru: Contemporary Playwright," *Journal of the Yokohama National University*, Sec. II, No. 33, December 1986, pp. 53-84; and "Out of the Sixties: Shimizu Kunio and Betsuyaku Minoru," *Journal of the Yokohama National University*, Sec. II, No. 35, October 1988, pp. 77-114.

Saeki suggests that if Kishida had pushed his dramaturgy to its logical extremes, he too would have become an Absurdist playwright. See Saeki, p. 432.

It is also interesting to note that Sueki Toshifumi, who has directed many of Betsuyaku's plays, has also been one of those most dedicated to reviving

He managed these feelings with a form of samurai stoicism that Fukuda calls "rigorism." At the same time, Kishida projected his feelings of paralysis, disintegration, and dislocation onto the stage in his dramatic works.

The vector of Kishida's plays is all-important. Kishida was projecting his own emotional reality onto the stage and not documenting in any objective fashion the impact of social change on individual psychology. His guiding principle, that "one does not write a play in order 'to say something'; one 'says something' in order for there to be a play," should be take seriously. In other words, although audiences and readers have found aspects of his work that resonate within them, it is because they have been able to identify with Kishida's personal emotional reality and not because he was describing theirs.

Kishida did in fact make a major contribution to the development of modern Japanese drama. That contribution was, as the playwright himself hoped it would be, in the area of language, in the development of a powerfully suggestive idiom for the stage. In preparing English versions of Kishida's plays, the translator cannot but be impressed by the precision, economy, and evocative power of Kishida's language.

The notion that Kishida singlehandedly created a modern theatre for Japan, however, is a gross exaggeration. Such an assertion not only distorts modern Japanese theatre history beyond recognition, but it ignores one of the most salient features of Kishida's work--that it was seldom performed.[89]

Watanabe Kazutami's revisionist portrait of Kishida is also unconvincing. Whatever Kishida's intentions and reservations about his wartime role, the overwhelming fact remains that he collaborated with the military establishment while other shingeki actors, directors, and playwrights who had resisted doing so languished in jail. The fact that "it would be possible to cite inflammatory writings by almost every recognized [Japanese] author,"[90] and that Kishida's prowar philippics were marginally less

---

Kishida's work.

[89] For example, *The Two Daughters of Mr. Sawa*, written in 1935, was not performed until 1951, when Tanaka Chikao directed the play for the Kurumiza troupe; and *The Diary of Fallen Leaves* was not performed until 1965, thirty-eight years after it was written, also by the Kurumiza.

[90] Donald Keene, "Japanese Writers and the Greater East Asia War," *Appreciations of Japanese Culture* (Tokyo and New York: Kodansha

hysterical than those of other intellectuals is simply not sufficient evidence to support Watanabe's conclusion that Kishida's behavior was really a form of wartime resistance.

In the final analysis, therefore, Kishida Kunio is a major but tragically flawed Japanese dramatist whose work commands our attention because of its richly evocative language.  Studying Kishida's plays can be a rewarding experience, but, as with the work of any other author, they should be read with a critical eye.

---

International, 1981), p. 302. Emphasis in the original.

# THE PLAYS

# AUTUMN IN THE TYROLS

(1924)

translated by

David G. Goodman
and
Kathleen Shigeta

*Characters:*
    Amano
    Stella
    Eliza

*Time:* Late autumn, 1920.

*Place:* Cortina, a small village near the Austro-Italian border.

*Dining room of the Hotel Pantheon. Seven o'clock in the evening. A fire is burning in the stove. Stella, in mourning clothes, has her eyes covered with a veil. While drinking coffee, she turns the pages of a book. Eliza stands beside her, holding the coffee pot. There is no one else in the room.*

ELIZA: You're leaving tomorrow. The day after tomorrow, Mr. Amano. Then this hotel will be deserted.

*Silence.*

STELLA: Do you know the train schedule?

ELIZA: My uncle hasn't come back yet. If you stayed one more day. . . .

STELLA: But I've already packed my bags. . . *(Pause.)* And if it started snowing, it would be such a nuisance.

ELIZA: You'll be all right. As long as the saffron in the pastures is blooming. *(Pause.)* But the weather has turned cold suddenly.

STELLA: And I thought I'd found a good spot to stay a while.

ELIZA: You're so lucky, traveling where you wish, saying, I'll stay here in the summer and here in the fall.

STELLA: I'd like to settle down if I could. *(Pause.)* I've been on this solitary journey for two years already. But wherever I go, I seem find something that doesn't suit my fancy. So I end up wandering about like this.

ELIZA: Mr. Amano was saying the same thing. It's been quite a while since he left his country, too, he says. He doesn't mind the cold, so he wants us to let him stay here. But we couldn't keep the hotel open just for him.

STELLA *(looking down at her book)*: Did he say he's going to Florence?

ELIZA: I don't know. I don't think he's decided. When I told him you were going to Sicily, he. . . .

STELLA *(smiling and looking up)*: What did he say?

*At this moment, Amano enters, holding a bouquet of saffron.*

ELIZA: You've been gone quite a while.

AMANO: I'm sorry to be late. *(He holds out the bouquet to Stella.)* Aren't they pretty?

STELLA *(smelling the flowers as she accepts the bouquet)*: For me? My! You're so thoughtful.

AMANO *(sitting down at the table, to Eliza)*: What are we having today?

ELIZA *(carrying in a plate)*: Trout. Then we have venison with chestnuts.

AMANO *(to Stella)*: Have you finished?

STELLA *(without taking her eyes off the book)*: Yes. But please, help yourself.

AMANO *(eating)*: It's delicious.

STELLA: Where did you go today?

AMANO *(with an ironic smile)*: The same old place.

STELLA *(trying to seem innocent)*: The castle?

AMANO: How did you guess?

STELLA: There's no great mystery. *(Pause.)* You like that sort of thing.

AMANO: What sort of thing?

STELLA: Watching people without being seen.

AMANO: But it seems I have been seen. Besides, it's a park. You don't do anything there that you don't want others to see.

STELLA: I'm not talking about propriety, I just love the color of the setting sun reflected on that mountain.

AMANO: Sublime, isn't it, that view?

STELLA: There's something mystical about it. The beauty of prayer.

AMANO: Nature in the Tyrols does have a certain religious beauty. Life does, too. You're a Christian, I suppose.

STELLA: I'm an atheist.

AMANO: But not without faith, I'm sure.

STELLA: What's the difference?

AMANO: I still don't know where you're from.

STELLA: All you have to do is look in the hotel register.

AMANO: That's just a hotel register. You're not American. . . . *(He gazes at her.)*

STELLA: Oh? *(She takes a last sip of coffee.)*

AMANO: I'm not much interested in the fact that I'm Japanese. And I don't really care where a person is from actually. I don't think our lives are so very different.

STELLA: That's true. *(She gets up from her chair and drapes herself onto the sofa.)* That's very true, I suppose.

*Silence.*

AMANO: It seems we are finally going to have to say good-bye.

STELLA *(as if she had been planning her response)*: We may never meet again.

ELIZA: You'll both come back here in the spring, won't you? I remember your saying so.

STELLA *(laughing)*: I said that to you.

AMANO: I wonder if I did. In any case, I have the sense we'll never meet again. It's not a bad feeling . . . provided we both feel that way.

STELLA *(half smiling)*: Indeed.

AMANO: Travelers are strange. They're frightfully sensitive about friendship. But they're almost laughably timid about getting emotionally involved.

STELLA: Getting emotionally involved . . . yes.

AMANO: Yes. I was convinced of it today.

STELLA *(listening)*: Eliza, didn't you hear that? At the window.

ELIZA *(hurrying to a window and opening the curtains slightly)*: Here?

STELLA *(amused)*: No, over here.

ELIZA *(she goes to the other window)*: You're teasing me!

STELLA *(laughing)*: No, I was right the first time. Listen.

ELIZA *(returning to the first window and this time opening it wide)*: Over here, Renatto. What? My uncle? He's gone into town. Not yet. Really? All right, where? Right this minute? Wait for me, I'll be there as soon as I can. *(She closes the window.)*

STELLA: Oh, do bring him in for once.

ELIZA *(preoccupied, to Amano)*: I hope you enjoy your dinner.

AMANO: Enjoy my dinner? That's a strange thing to say. At least bring the rest of the meal out, won't you. I'll serve myself.

ELIZA *(carrying out the next dish and coffee)*: You really don't mind?

AMANO: I could tell your uncle.

ELIZA: If you do, I'll just run away. *(She spins around.)*

STELLA: Of course you will. Go to him now. Your handsome lieutenant awaits you impatiently, rattling his sword!

ELIZA *(hesitating)*: Let him wait for a change.

STELLA: Oh my, it's a little late to be taking that attitude.

ELIZA *(straightening her hair as she edges toward the door)*: When my uncle comes back, tell him I've already gone to bed.

AMANO: Where?

ELIZA *(running out the door)*: You're terrible!

AMANO: This summer I heard a story from a German officer. During the war, there was a company of school teachers occupying the French countryside. On the day they were scheduled to pull out, all the girls in the village lined the road and wept.

STELLA: What a terrible story.

AMANO: Really?

STELLA: And what's more. . . . *(Thinking better of it, she suddenly holds her tongue.)*

AMANO: You don't seem to take emotional involvement all that seriously.

STELLA:  All that seriously?

AMANO:  Do you?

STELLA:  How un-Japanese you are!

AMANO:  What do you mean by that?

STELLA:  Never mind.  You never talk about Japan.

*Amano smiles but does not respond.*

STELLA:  You don't like talking about your country, do you?

AMANO:  And you?

STELLA:  Nagasaki is a nice place, isn't it?

AMANO:  What difference does it make?

STELLA:  No difference.

AMANO:  I'm more interested in knowing where you're from.

STELLA:  What did you say before?

AMANO:  I only ask because you're so intent on hiding it.  I have no particular preference that you be an Italian rather than an Austrian.

STELLA:  I know you don't.  *(Pause.)*  On the other hand, who knows? Why don't you try guessing?

AMANO:  I will, but let me look at your eyes first.  *(He stands up and goes over to the stove.)*

STELLA:  Be my guest.  Look as much as you like.

AMANO:  Then lift your veil.

STELLA:  I'll do no such thing.

AMANO:  See what I mean.  You like being that way, don't you?

STELLA:  You mustn't say such things.

AMANO *(still with his back to Stella)*:  Your eyes through a veil are like lips that don't speak.  I'm sure your eyes would speak volumes if I could only see them.

STELLA:  How very inquisitive you are!

AMANO:  Is there something wrong with that?  *(Pause.)*  You are always weeping.

*Silence. Stella says nothing.*

AMANO:  Your tears flow from dream to dream.

STELLA *(with a sigh)*:  My dreams . . . do you know what my dreams are like?

AMANO *(turning to her)*:  Your dreams?  They're dreams that envelop all reality like a mist.  You travel: that, for you, is a dream.  You read a book, another dream.  You fall in love: that, too, is a dream.

STELLA:  Please wait.  The reason I'm talking to you like this. . . .  No, that's not true.  The point is, I'm still living.

AMANO:  You're living within your dreams.

STELLA:  One dream anyway.

AMANO: A memory no doubt, a sad, exquisite one. A not uncommon one.

STELLA: How pleased you are with yourself.

AMANO: Not in the least. *(Seriously.)* Actually, I was describing myself.

*Silence.*

STELLA: I thought you'd say that.

AMANO: I didn't have to.

STELLA: Then let's talk about something else.

AMANO: Something else? Good idea. *(Pause.)* That book you're always reading, what is it?

STELLA: This? *(About to show him the book in her hand, she hastily hides it behind her back instead.)* What difference does it make? Please don't ask me any more questions. I refuse to answer.

AMANO: Then, we can't talk. *(Pause.)* This is the first opportunity we've had like this. As soon as we finish a meal, you always avoid people and lose yourself in reading or meditation. I haven't been able to get near you except in this dining room. *(Pause.)* This is our last night together after all.

STELLA: Our last night together. That, too, is a game of the imagination.

AMANO: All right. But couldn't we play this imaginary game more enjoyably, just the two of us? Let me remind you that tomorrow morning when your coach carries you through the mountains, I will disappear forever from your dreams.

STELLA: Are you serious?

AMANO: Travelers' hearts are linked by a friendship that's not bound by commitments. You hold a hand aware that you may never hold it again, and in that hand lies the sense of freedom that comes with traveling. *(Pause.)* Here we are in the heart of the Tyrolean mountains, two people who haven't even spoken to each other about themselves: wouldn't it be amusing if we spent the night like long-lost lovers who have vowed never to meet again? *(Pause.)* You would be dreaming. There would be another person, a man, also dreaming. Their dreams would coincide. That would be it. *(Pause.)* Two people meet in a dream, fall in love in a dream. Well? Would you like to try that kind of love, just once?

STELLA: I prefer to dream alone.

AMANO: You dream of whatever you like, and I'll do the same.

STELLA: And then?

AMANO: The man you love would be me.

STELLA: And I would be the woman you love?

AMANO: Not you and I. Your lover and you. My lover and I. We are together here now.

STELLA *(amused)*: And then?

AMANO: I think you know what happens after that.

STELLA: Oh, so we're playing house. Play-acting.

AMANO: Playing house, but in earnest. Play-acting in earnest. Come, you love me.

STELLA: But. . . .

AMANO: Let's just say you do.

STELLA: And you love me?

AMANO: That's right. Imagining something rationally is preferable to experiencing it awkwardly. Look, your lover is kneeling at your feet, like so. *(He does not kneel.)*

*Stella laughs.*

AMANO: Don't laugh.

STELLA: Let's put some wood in the stove.

AMANO *(stoking the stove)*: I have my ear to your heart, trying not to miss the tiniest murmur. *(He draws near Stella.)* I fill my lungs with your breath. You can feel it. That's the dream. Let's find out what happens next. *(He draws even closer to her and sits down.)*

STELLA *(in a tremulous voice)*: You're strange.

AMANO: Strange? I'm only strange because you think I am. Adults aren't allowed to watch children's games. *(Whispering in her ear.)* I love you. I love you from the bottom of my heart. My soul has been captivated by your beauty. How trite! Well, listen anyway. I don't want to disturb your dream, nor do I wish to disturb mine. The joy of the moment when you've consummated your love doesn't last forever. The moment I possess you, I want to lose you. Do you understand what I'm saying? You don't? The moment I think that you love me, the moment that your lips touch mine, that moment will be the happiest dream in my life. First, squeeze my hand. *(He takes Stella's hand.)*

STELLA *(trembling)*: This is a play. We are only play-acting?

AMANO *(trying to take both her hands)*: Don't be afraid. . . .

STELLA *(brushing his hands aside)*: No, stop it. You mustn't appear in my dreams. That's what I'm most. . . . It's a man like you . . . who will wake me from my reverie.

AMANO: I'm just a passerby. Someone who shined your shoes at the curbside. The man who gave up his seat for you on the train. The man who picked up the handkerchief you dropped on the theatre floor.

STELLA *(with emotion)*: You don't know what's in a woman's heart.

AMANO *(taking her hand)*: It's impossible to read the heart of an indifferent woman.

STELLA *(as if she's reconsidered, she squeezes his hand)*: All right. Let's perform this little play. But you mustn't forget your promise. Just tonight. All right? Only for tonight. *(As if intoxicated.)* Do go on. I feel so lonely. For some reason I feel lonely tonight. I feel so lonely, as if the dream I've been living all this time were coming to an end. Please. Do say something, quickly.

AMANO: First, let me see your eyes, just once. Lift your veil, please? *(He places his hands on her shoulders and draws her closer.)* Why are you crying?

*Silence. Stella removes her veil and wipes her tears.*

AMANO: What's so sad?

STELLA: I'm not sad. It's just a habit. *(Looking toward him, she smiles.)*

AMANO: Yes, yes! Those are the eyes! *(He embraces her.)*

STELLA: Hold me tighter! My lover is embracing me. *(Gradually warming.)* I love you so much! Hold me tighter. Such a peaceful night. Just the way it was that night long ago. Darling, you're trembling. *(Pause.)* Don't deceive me! You're awful! You said this would only be for tonight!

AMANO *(realizing)*: You'll be mine forever. I won't let you go, not until the flesh of this arm crumbles from the bone.

STELLA: Don't say such a gruesome thing. Say, until my blond hair has turned to gray. Until my eyes begin to fade.

AMANO: My hair isn't blond.

STELLA: That doesn't matter. It's only a metaphor. Don't be angry. You're Japanese. My mother was born in Nagasaki. Her name was Hama.

*Amano looks at her in surprise.*

STELLA: Why are you so surprised? Because I have dark eyes? I can't help it. Do you dislike dark eyes?

AMANO *(changing his demeanor)*: Stella, tell me the truth. What you said just now, it's not a joke, is it?

STELLA: Please, you're frightening me.

AMANO *(firmly)*: That's enough play-acting. I'm asking you again, tell me who you are.

STELLA: You're a strange person.

AMANO: Don't you understand how I feel?

STELLA: It doesn't matter whether I do or not. It's only a play we're acting out. *(Silence.)* Let's stop being so serious and have the rest of our dream.  If I change my mind, it'll be too late.

AMANO:  Don't misunderstand me.  But now I think I know the real you.
When I looked into your eyes for the first time just now, I felt as if I
were seeing my whole life spread before me.  But I can't be satisfied
with just one moment of bliss.

STELLA *(throwing her arms around his neck)*:  Never mind all that.  Just
come closer.  When was it?  There was this villa overlooking the
Rhine.  I think it was a villa.  Anyway, the first night we stayed
there, we'd been out the whole day  boating, until late.  That night,
you were so drunk.  Why did you drink so much?  Did I make you
drunk?  *(Suddenly she embraces Amano and kisses him on the lips.)*
Don't just sit there without saying a word.  *(Pause.)* My bedroom was
next to yours.  When I opened my window, you opened yours.  Then
what happened?

AMANO *(resigned)*:  I coughed.

STELLA:  Yes, yes, that's right.  And I?

AMANO:  You closed the window.

STELLA:  I did not!  I sang a song.  *(She hums.)*

AMANO:  I remember that song.

STELLA:  Yes.  And then the balcony.  It was such a peaceful night.  The
stars were out.  You were so funny, like a child.  Remember?

AMANO:  And after that, our trip to the Tyrols.  An autumn night in
Cortina.  Instead of stars, look, a fire burning in the stove.

STELLA:  Not so fast.  You've always been impatient.

AMANO:  I'm not interested in what happened in between.  Tomorrow I'll
go with you to Sicily.

STELLA:  To Sicily?  There are snakes there, you know.

AMANO:  Snakes?  I suppose there are snakes.  You liked to walk on the
cold marble floors in your bare feet.

STELLA:  And I liked to let my hair be teased by the wind in the orange
grove.  Yes, that's right, you played the flute so well.

AMANO *(with a gloomy expression)*:  The flute?  All right, I'll play the
flute.

*Silence.*

STELLA:  What's the matter?  Did I say something?

AMANO:  No.  *(Pause. Then coldly)*:  Who are you talking to?  Who's
good at playing the flute?  *(As if it had just dawned on him.)* What a
fool I am, asking a question like that.  I won't do it  again.  *(Pause.)*
But please say something.  And say it to me.  Aren't you sleepy?

STELLA *(as if she wants to laugh)*:  You still doubt me, don't you?  Go
ahead, take me wherever you like.  Go ahead, do whatever satisfies

you.

AMANO: That's not what I meant. I didn't want to wake you from your dream. I just wanted to make your heart speak to me unfettered by the dream. Now, there you go again, looking away from me. *(He puts his hand on her shoulder.)* What do your eyes see now? Who are they seeing? Stella, can you hear me?

STELLA *(in a tiny voice)*: Please be quiet. *(She is silent.)* Why am I like this, I wonder?

AMANO: See how strange you are? What do you want?

STELLA: I don't want anything.

AMANO: Then you don't want me.

STELLA: You? Who are you? No, you be quiet. I'll think this thing out for myself.

AMANO: You mustn't think. You must abandon yourself, do as your emotions dictate. Don't you realize how much you torment yourself, chasing a distant phantom?

STELLA: I'm not in the least bit tormented. *(She is silent. Then, almost desperately)*: If only you would get out of my sight. If only you'd be quiet! Better still, if only I had never met you. . . . *(Her voice gradually becomes fainter.)*

AMANO: Then what do you want me to do? *(Triumphantly)*: Do you want me to die?

STELLA *(categorically)*: Yes, die!

AMANO *(taking her hand and leaping to his feet)*: Oh, thank you! I will give my life for you. In return, your heart shall be mine.

STELLA *(interrupting, she rises)*: Be my guest. If you can take it with you.

*Silence.*

AMANO: Stella. . . .

STELLA: I wonder what time it is. *(She goes to the window, opens the curtain, and looks outside.)* It's terrible foggy again.

AMANO: And the fire's gone out in the stove.

STELLA: Perhaps it's time we retire.

*Silence.*

AMANO: Stella. . . . *(He rises.)*

STELLA: Yes, I suppose it is better to be alone, if you're only going to dream.

AMANO *(laughing bitterly)*: It's only when you awake that you want someone to play with.

STELLA: Don't you let anything disturb your dream either. Good night.

AMANO: My dream seems on the verge of collapsing.

STELLA *(laughing)*: In that case, come and we'll play at dreaming again. You know the way.

AMANO: Don't go far.

STELLA *(approaching him)*: I'll see you tomorrow morning. *(She holds out her hand to be kissed.)* I'll be expecting you to come and say good-bye.

AMANO *(kissing Stella's hand)*: That depends on what I'm dreaming.

STELLA *(laughing)*: Yes, of course. *(Cautiously withdrawing her hand.)* Good night.

AMANO: Good night

*Stella exits without looking back. Amano watches her leave.*

*Outside, a hoarse voice cries, "Eliza! Eliza!"*

*Silence.*

*Curtain.*

# PAPER BALLOON

## (1925)

translated by

Richard McKinnon

*Characters:*
    Husband
    Wife

*Time:*
    A bright Sunday afternoon.

*Place:*
    The sitting-room facing the garden.

HUSBAND *(reading a newspaper on the veranda as he sits in a rattan chair)*: "The modern village of Mejiro, recently acclaimed as a Los Angeles in miniature by Mr. Turner, Managing Director of the Fuller Building Supplies Company, U.S.A., has today become an elegant and beautiful residential area."

WIFE *(sitting on a cushion near the veranda as she knits)*: What is that about?

HUSBAND *(reading on)*: "The area which covers 40,000 *tsubo* is ideally situated: Streets are laid out systematically. A sewage system, running water, electric heat--the most hygienic facilities are provided. Tennis courts have been installed. There are many pretty little bungalow-type houses. There are houses that are built in the impressive style of Frank Lloyd Wright. There are even houses built in the graceful, cottage-style Japanese architecture. This residential area is set in cheerful surroundings. Situated on high ground from where one can view Mt. Fuji, it is heavily covered with trees." *(Tosses the newspaper aside)*: Look, how about a walk?

WIFE: Never mind. Why don't you go ahead and go over to the Kawakamis.

HUSBAND: I really don't have to go.

WIFE: The mood has to strike me just right or I can't get interested.

HUSBAND: For a walk you mean?

WIFE: A walk or anything else. *(Pause.)*

HUSBAND: "A walk or anything else." But do you have anything else to do?

WIFE: No, isn't that all right?

HUSBAND: Sure.

WIFE: Why don't you go visit the Kawakamis without worrying about me?

HUSBAND: I don't feel like it any more.

WIFE: Oh, go on.

HUSBAND: No, I'm not going. I want to stay with you. Don't you understand?

WIFE: Sorry, I understand all too perfectly. *(Pause.)*

HUSBAND: Ho, hum. So this is the way I spend my occasional Sundays off.

WIFE: I guess so.

HUSBAND (*picks up the paper again but isn't really interested in reading*): I think it would be fun if some newspaper offered a prize for the best answer to the question of what to do in situations like this.

WIFE: I'll send in an answer.

HUSBAND (*still looking at the paper, showing little interest*): What will you say?

WIFE: What's the question?

HUSBAND: The question? Well, the question will say, "How would you spend your Sundays when you have been married a year?"

WIFE: That's too vague.

HUSBAND: What's vague about it? All right, how would you put it?

WIFE: How to keep the wife from getting bored on Sundays?

HUSBAND: And how not to inconvenience the husband at the same time?

WIFE: All right.

HUSBAND: Do you have a good idea?

WIFE: Why, I sure do. As soon as the wife gets up in the morning, she will take a bath, put on her makeup, get dressed and then say, "I'm off to visit a friend of mine for a while."

HUSBAND: What happens then?

WIFE: Then her husband is sure to look displeased.

HUSBAND: There's nothing certain about that.

WIFE: I am talking about you.

HUSBAND: When did I look displeased?

WIFE: Don't you?

HUSBAND: Well, let's let that go. What do you do then?

WIFE: He looks displeased, you see. Then this is what I would say: I'm not really very anxious to go, but it would be awkward if they found out later that I had stayed home doing nothing. You see, every time I see her she keeps asking me to come over to her place. "If it's a Sunday my husband will be at home. Why don't you and I go see a play together," she says. Since you're going to be home anyway, I thought I might as well go today. But of course if you have other plans, I would say and gently sound you out. Very indirectly, you understand.

HUSBAND: Yes, very indirectly. No. I wouldn't mind, but what would I do about lunch, with you gone.

WIFE: I prepared your lunch already.

HUSBAND: What about supper?

WIFE: I'll stop at the Azumaya's on my way out, and ask them to deliver a big bowl of rice with chicken and egg on top.

HUSBAND: Oh, not that again. I suppose you're going to be late.

WIFE: Well, I can't be sure. But when ten o'clock comes around will you get out the bedding and go to bed?

HUSBAND: Do you have any money?

WIFE: As a matter of fact, I'm completely out.

HUSBAND: Well, you'd better take this, then.

WIFE: Thank you.

HUSBAND: It's getting chilly at night. Take your muffler along.

WIFE: Yes, I will.

HUSBAND: Now then. I guess I'll leisurely read a book. Say, would you get the fire started for my bath before you go? Now if I have any visitors, I suppose we still have some cookies left from the last time. I'll skip shaving today. Ho, hum. What a relaxing Sunday.

*Wife silently looks down.*

HUSBAND: What's the matter?

WIFE: You're no good.

HUSBAND: Why?

WIFE: Because.

HUSBAND (*tossing the paper aside*): All right. Then what would you do in such a case if you were the husband?

WIFE: In what case?

HUSBAND: Would you stop her?

WIFE: I'd certainly try to stop her somehow!

HUSBAND: What would you say to her?

WIFE: I'd say something like, "If you really don't have to go, how about my taking you to the theatre?"

HUSBAND: I see. What if he suggested that?

WIFE: She ought to go.

HUSBAND: Fine, if she will. But if she didn't want to go, then what? Or even if she did, if the circumstances made it impossible, like today for instance.

WIFE: Why couldn't we substitute the movies for the theatre?

HUSBAND: Movies? Why that's not something a husband and wife go together to see.

WIFE: Why not?

HUSBAND: Ask anyone.

WIFE: That's what's wrong with you. I'm different from other girls.

HUSBAND: Sure you're different. That's all the more reason why it would be unwise.

WIFE: What are you talking about?

HUSBAND: Well, it seems better not to have stopped her, if she had wanted to go out.

WIFE: I guess you're right. So why don't you go, to the Kawakami's or wherever else.

HUSBAND: My, you're persistent, aren't you? What was it that you said this morning? When I told you that I was going over to visit Kawakami you said, "You keep mentioning Mr. Kawakami's name, as if you didn't see him every day at your office. Why do you long for him so much? Is there any reason why you can't stay at home on a Sunday, at least? What's the point of my being here?

WIFE: What if I did say so?

HUSBAND: Nothing. The question is what is the point of your being here.

WIFE *(somewhat peevishly)*: Well, is something wrong with my being here?

HUSBAND: But there are ways and ways of being here. I read the newspaper, and you start knitting. I heave a sigh and you heave a sigh. I yawn and then you yawn. I. . . .

WIFE: That's why I suggested that we go out somewhere, and then you hedge about this way and that. . . .

HUSBAND: Yes, yes. I understand. But surely we didn't get married just so we could go somewhere on Sundays. We ought to be able to get on more cheerfully even if we stayed home.

WIFE: That's because you don't talk.

HUSBAND: Talk? What is there to talk about?

WIFE: Talk is not being; it is an act of doing.

HUSBAND: What on earth! Philosophizing? All right, so let's say that talk is an act of doing. But what about you? You say nothing yourself.

WIFE: That's because you tell me to shut up.

HUSBAND: That's because you talk when I'm doing something.

WIFE: That's not true. You say that even after we are in bed.

HUSBAND: But I'm sorry.

WIFE *(softly)*: Actually I am quite content to be at your side saying nothing. If you'd only pay a little more attention to me, I could wish for no one better.

HUSBAND *(looking triumphant)*: What's for supper?

WIFE *(spiritedly)*: Nothing definite. It all depends on your grade.

HUSBAND *(not quite equal to her mood)*: You are still just a high school girl, aren't you?

WIFE: Meaning what? I've always felt that going to the theatre or eating out is fine for Sundays if one has that much leeway. But that's still only secondary in importance. Surely there are any number of things that one can enjoy as a family. Take our garden, for example. Why, it's a disgrace. If you'd lend me a hand I could so easily have a decent bed of flowers. Just imagine the cosmos in full bloom. It would look beautiful even from the street.

HUSBAND: That's what I mean about your being a high school girl.

WIFE: In that case you're a grade school boy.

HUSBAND *(laughing)*: Is there really something of a school boy in me, now?

WIFE: Sure there is.

HUSBAND: Look, let's go for a walk.

WIFE: It's too late now.

HUSBAND: Oh, just around the neighborhood.

WIFE: Where? Inokashira Park?

HUSBAND: Or even Tamagawa.

WIFE: Let's wait until there is more time. To make it real fun we ought to make an occasion of it and have lunch out somewhere.

HUSBAND: How much money do you have?

WIFE: Oh, let's not talk about that today.

HUSBAND *(counting on his fingers)*: Sixteen, seventeen, eighteen, nineteen.

WIFE: We really ought to have everything ready in the morning, and plan to be off as soon as we are through breakfast.

HUSBAND: Yes, with plans all laid out the night before.

WIFE: That's right. To have a definite idea as to where we are going.

HUSBAND: It would be fun, wouldn't it, to take a day trip to Kamakura?

WIFE: I have some places I'd like to go.

HUSBAND: Let's see now. There is an eight-something train leaving Tokyo station in the morning.

WIFE: Second class, mind you.

HUSBAND: Naturally. What we ought to do is to get there early and occupy the two seats near the window facing each other. I would put my walking stick and your parasol up on the luggage shelf like this. . . .

WIFE: No, I would rather carry mine.

HUSBAND: I see. Those coming in after us would see us and try to sit as near to us as possible, saying to themselves, "Oh, boy, look at them at it."

WIFE: Oh, silly!

HUSBAND: The train starts to move.

WIFE: Would you open the window?

HUSBAND: Smoke will come in. See that over there. That's the ruins of the Hama Detached Palace.

WIFE: My, is that so?

HUSBAND: Shinagawa, Shinagawa! All passengers taking the Yamate line must transfer.

WIFE: Already? I want to buy some caramels.

HUSBAND: O.K. Hey, bring me some caramels.

WIFE: Would you like some?

HUSBAND: I guess so. We just passed Ōmori Station. We should be able to see the company president's home pretty soon.

WIFE: Is that the one? My, what a skimpy house!

HUSBAND: We'll skip Kamata and Kawasaki, and here we are in Yokohama. Well, we have no business here either. Hodogaya, Tozuka, and we are in Ōfuna at last.

WIFE: I want to buy some sandwiches.

HUSBAND: O.K. Hey, bring me some sandwiches.

WIFE: Would you like some?

HUSBAND: I guess so.

WIFE: Wait, now. Don't be so greedy. Leave some for me.

HUSBAND: Now, get ready to leave. Put your clogs back on. . . .

WIFE: I never had them off, for goodness sake!

HUSBAND: I suppose the first place to go is the Hachiman Shrine. Do you know about this shrine?

WIFE: Of course I do. I'd rather go to the seashore, though. How about you?

HUSBAND: That would be all right, too. Let me see. . . .

WIFE: Why not get a cab.

HUSBAND: That's an idea. Hey, taxi! Now you go first.

WIFE: That's very kind of you.

HUSBAND: Well, I guess I'll light up a cigarette.

WIFE: But first tell the driver where to go.

HUSBAND: What's the matter with saying, "To the seashore."

WIFE: That sounds a bit strange. "Driver, to the Beach Hotel."

HUSBAND: Won't the Beach Hotel be closed?

WIFE: You know it isn't.

HUSBAND: All right. To the Beach Hotel. Toot, toot!

WIFE: What's all that for. We're already there.

HUSBAND: Goodness, already? Would you take us to a room with a good view?

WIFE: The dining room would do.

HUSBAND: Of course. So, why don't you order something.

WIFE: How about you?

HUSBAND: Anything would do.

WIFE: Two glasses of fruit juice. Be sure they are good and cold.

HUSBAND: Waitress, we are going for a little stroll. There's still some time before noon. We'll be back by twelve, so have something good ready for us.

WIFE: That's the spirit.

HUSBAND: Oh, one more thing. Are there any good rooms available, rooms with a *salle de bains*? We intend to stay here for a while.

WIFE: *Salle de bains*? Oh, you mean a bathroom.

HUSBAND: Sh! Oh, fine. We'll take that. No, we don't have to look at it first. Oh, by the way, doesn't your hotel have airplane service?

WIFE: Please!

HUSBAND: No? Oh, well, it can't be helped. Let's walk. Now for my walking stick.

WIFE: Are you sure you didn't leave it in the train again?

HUSBAND: I handed it to the bellhop. Ah, there it is!

WIFE: Which way shall we go?

HUSBAND: That island over there is Enoshima.

WIFE: What a lovely view!

HUSBAND: Watch your step. You'll fall. Let me hold your hand.

WIFE: People would look at us.

HUSBAND: That's too bad for them. Tired? Well, let's sit down and rest a bit, or, if you'd rather, we might go bathing.

WIFE: I think I will.

HUSBAND: Go ahead. Hmm. You look very trim in a bathing suit. Don't go too far out.

WIFE: Don't worry.

HUSBAND: Wait, wait. Stand right there. I'll take a picture of you. Ready? Hey, this is wonderful. (*Becoming more and more excited*): I've never seen you so pretty! Just look at that figure! What a marvelous complexion! Stay right where you are. Did you have your hair that long? And your bosom, so round and soft! Why, you're smiling. Look this way. Heavens, were these your eyes, and those lips? (*He shouts, forgetting everything.*)

WIFE (*raising her head for the first time, as if about to take him to task*): Please!

*Long silence.*

HUSBAND: Come over here.

*Wife just smiles.*

HUSBAND (*extending his hands*): Come over here.

WIFE: No.

HUSBAND: Oh, come on now. Come over here, I say.

*Wife rises and takes her husband's hands, swinging them.*

WIFE: There's no middle ground in you, is there?

HUSBAND: How do you mean? *(He tries to draw his wife to him.)*

WIFE: Let me go!

HUSBAND *(holding his wife's hands)*: Won't there be a time when you will be tired of me, tired of holding hands with me like this?

WIFE: How about you?

HUSBAND: The fact is I am beginning to like this very much, this holding hands, and when I think of being left alone without you I get so worried I don't know what to do. This, too, is a fact.

WIFE: Which one represents the truth?

HUSBAND: Both. *(Pause)*: That's why I feel that something is wrong. But I can't help it. *(Pause)*: So you sit and knit by me in silence. Are you really satisfied with that? I see no reason why you should be. Maybe in my absence there are times when you sit and brood all by yourself in the corner of a room somewhere. Away from home, I often picture you in my mind sitting there looking lonely. Don't you get sick and tired of leading the kind of life we do in which all we think about is how to spend my less-than-hundred-yen pay check in as grand a manner as possible? Maybe you are resigned to the situation, feeling that nothing is gained by talking this way. But I know that you have your ideals, and I'd like to know what you think about it at this point? Aren't you wondering what will become of us as we go on living like this? Am I wrong? Or are you dreaming again the dream that you had as a young girl?

WIFE: You are being foolish. *(She tries to smile, but she begins to cry.)*

HUSBAND: People are all fools. They don't know about themselves. Oh, let's cut out this kind of talk.

WIFE: I haven't cried like this for a long time.

HUSBAND: I go out visiting on a Sunday, leaving you all alone. You're unhappy about it. It's to be expected. Of course you'd like a change once in a while. Why should I make a fuss about movies! Let's plan to go after supper, huh?

*Wife nods.*

HUSBAND: Fine. You want to go take a quick bath?

WIFE *(wiping her tears away)*: No, I'll skip it today.

HUSBAND: Why?

WIFE: Why don't you? You haven't had one in three days.

HUSBAND: Well, I've got a touch of cold. Oh, I think I'll skip it today. Let me see; it's 3:30 now, I think I'll go out for a while before supper instead.

WIFE *(sitting down on her cushion again, resentfully)*: Where are you going?

HUSBAND: Oh, I'll be back in no time.

*Wife stares at her husband, starts to say something, but then suddenly looks down.*

WIFE: All right.

HUSBAND *(sheepishly)*: I'm not going to Kawakami's.

WIFE *(embarrassed)*: It doesn't matter at all.

HUSBAND *(kneeling down beside his wife)*: I suppose you think I'm going out to play billiards.

WIFE *(looking the other way)*: Don't mind me. Run along.

HUSBAND: Are you angry?

*Wife begins crying again.*

HUSBAND *(at a loss)*: What's the matter, anyway?

WIFE: I'm sorry. It was my mistake.

HUSBAND: What do you mean, "mistake"? We are going to the movies afterwards, don't you see?

WIFE *(heaving a sigh)*: I understand.

HUSBAND: You understand what?

WIFE: I might as well face up to it.

HUSBAND: To what?

WIFE: I'm sorry.

HUSBAND: Look, something's wrong with you.

WIFE: It's funny, you know. Other wives say they can relax and enjoy things when their husbands are out of the house. But it seemed so odd to me.

HUSBAND: Sure it's odd.

WIFE: But, it's no longer odd to me now.

HUSBAND: What?

WIFE: Men, I guess, are after all made to leave home in the morning and return in the evening.

*Husband smiles sardonically.*

WIFE: I wonder why men make such a fuss over the fact that they are staying home, as if they were doing you a favor. Women I suppose just can't stand for that.

HUSBAND: I'm not making a fuss about it.

WIFE: Anyway, if you have somewhere to go, go, run along. It makes me feel a whole lot better.

*Husband sits down in his chair again and starts reading the paper.*

WIFE: I'm afraid to face Sundays.

HUSBAND: So am I.

*Pause.*

WIFE: You are spoiling me too much. *(She takes up her knitting.)*

HUSBAND: No, I can't say I am.

WIFE: But you are, really.

HUSBAND: Complicated, isn't it?

WIFE: See how they do it in other families.

HUSBAND: I know how they do it.

WIFE: Follow suit.

HUSBAND: I can't.

WIFE: Women are given to taking advantage of situations, you know?

HUSBAND: I know that.

WIFE: Well, just so long as you do.

*Long pause.*

HUSBAND: Actually, I think we are getting along better than many.

WIFE: Just a little more effort, I guess.

HUSBAND: You mean money?

WIFE: Oh, no.

*Long silence.*

HUSBAND: How about getting a dog?

WIFE: Won't a bird be better?

*Long silence.*

> *Husband yawns.*
> *Wife yawns.*
> *Pause.*

HUSBAND: Would you like me to tell you a story?

WIFE: Yes, do.

HUSBAND: Long, long ago there was a boy and girl. The boy, as soon as he finished school, went to work in an office. The girl was still in high school. Every morning the two saw each other at a suburban bus stop. In time they greeted each other. When the boy got there first he waited for the girl to come. When the girl arrived first, she . . .

WIFE *(taking it away from him)*: Went on ahead.

HUSBAND *(matter of factly)*: There were times like that.

*At this point, the voice of a little girl is heard crying out: "Oh, dear!" A big paper balloon rolls into the garden.*

*Husband, tossing the newspaper aside, steps off the verandah into the garden and picks up the balloon.*

WIFE *(to herself)*: Chieko-chan at home today?

*Husband quietly starts tossing the balloon.*

WIFE: Don't do that. *(In a loud voice)*: Chieko-chan, come over here.

I'll toss the balloon with you.

*Husband continues to toss the balloon eagerly.*

*Wife rises, brings her clogs around from the front entrance, and then comes out into the garden.*

WIFE: No, no, don't hit it so hard. *(She calls to the little girl who apparently is on the other side of the fence.)* I am ready to play with you now. *(As she says this she manages to snatch the balloon away from her husband.)* Chieko-chan come around from the front.

HUSBAND *(chasing his wife, impatiently)*: Now, let me have a turn. Look here, I tell you. . . .

*Curtain.*

# CLOUDBURST

## (1926)

translated by

Richard McKinnon

*Characters*:
  Tomoko
  Yuzuru, Tomoko's husband
  Tsuneko, Tomoko's younger sister
  A housekeeper

*Time*:
  One June afternoon.

*Place*:
  A Western style study which doubles as a parlor.

*Tomoko dashes into the room as she removes her apron. The housekeeper follows close behind. She evidently has something to say.*

TOMOKO: That's fine. I like it that way. *(She hands her apron to the housekeeper, and sits at the desk.)* You are through with everything but handkerchiefs, aren't you? Good. Do them when you have time, but be sure not to get the iron too hot. Oh, and another thing--but first would you do an errand for me? I want you to go to the grocery store down the street and see if they have any strawberries. If they don't have any good ones there, would you go over to the store opposite the railroad station and get a box of their choice ones?

HOUSEKEEPER: How much should I spend?

TOMOKO: It doesn't matter, as long as they are really good. *(She picks up a pen and starts rummaging around in the drawer.)* I am going to write a postcard now. Will you mail it on your way out? You'd better get ready. *(She starts writing.)* Now, let me see.

*The housekeeper leaves the room. A long interval.*

TOMOKO: Oh, Miss Yoshizawa! Would you hand me the postcard that came this morning? It ought to be on the letter rack. It's a picture postcard.

HOUSEKEEPER *(brings a postcard)*: Is this the one?

TOMOKO *(takes it without looking)*: Yes, that's it. *(Looks at it.)* No, this isn't it. There was one that came this morning. *(Chuckles to herself as she reads the first card handed to her.)* Just imagine! *(The housekeeper leaves the room also in smiles.)* It has a picture of the seashore. It says Kamagôri on it.

*Housekeeper appears with the picture postcard. She is looking at it.*

TOMOKO *(grabs it away)*: Here. Yes, this is the one all right. *(Pause)*: "We are both delighted with this place, and plan to stay here for four or five days . . . " Well, how about that!

HOUSEKEEPER: Did you say something?

TOMOKO: Nothing at all. You had better hurry.

*The housekeeper leaves the room.*

TOMOKO *(continues to write)*: " . . . Have a good time while you still can. Remember me to your husband." Well, that takes care of that. Miss Yoshizawa, will you take this card with you? Aren't you ready yet? Oh, that's right. Will you check the bath before you leave? It's almost time for my husband to come home.

HOUSEKEEPER *(from the inner room)*: The bath is all ready.

TOMOKO: Good. *(Pause.)* What are you doing then?

HOUSEKEEPER: I'm redoing my sash.

TOMOKO: What do you need to bother with a sash for every time you go out? It's just a short walk.

*The front door is heard opening. Tomoko goes out.*

*Pause.*

*Yuzuru enters the room, mechanically picks up the picture postcard on the desk and reads it.*

TOMOKO *(entering the room)*: Would you like to take your bath now?

*Yuzuru remains silent. A moment later he goes to the inner room.*

*Tomoko slumps into a chair with a look of disappointment. But soon she recovers her cheerfulness and gets up.*

YUZURU'S VOICE: Hey.

*Tomoko goes to the inner room without a word.*

*Long interval.*

*A woman's voice is heard at the front door: "Hello." A second voice, the obviously startled voice of Tomoko, follows: "My! . . . "*

TOMOKO'S VOICE: What happened? Why did you come back? Are you alone? *(Pause.)* I read your card just this morning. *(Pause.)* Yes. You said you were staying there four or five days, so I didn't expect you so soon. *(Pause.)* Is that so? Come on in, anyway. *(Pause.)* He just got back a few minutes ago. *(Pause.)* Of course, it is all right.

*First Tomoko, then Tsuneko enter the room. Tsuneko looks a little tired.*

TOMOKO: Something happened, didn't it? What are you giggling about, silly?

TSUNEKO *(sits in a chair)*: Let me catch my breath a minute. I came straight from the station.

TOMOKO: Well, tell me about it?

TSUNEKO: You mean about that person? *(Smiles significantly)*: I'll tell you in a moment. *(Sighs)*: You are sure I'm not intruding?

TOMOKO *(looking at Tsuneko questioningly)*: Really, Tsune, what is the matter with you, just giggling like that?

TSUNEKO: Don't be so impatient!

*Tsuneko looks away from her sister and quickly pulls out a handkerchief. Her eyes are brimming with tears. She tries to force a laugh, as if struck by the ridiculousness of her present situation. But she can continue the pretense no longer, and holding her handkerchief to her eyes she bursts into tears.)*

TOMOKO *(at a loss)*: My, you're funny! What on earth is the matter? *(She places her hand on her sister's shoulder.)*

*Tsuneko does not react.*

TOMOKO: Crying won't help a bit. Is something the matter with you? Tell me quickly.

TSUNEKO: I'm sorry. When I saw you I suddenly felt so sad. *(Pause.)* I had pretty much made up my mind to say nothing about it, to bear with it in silence. But, I just can't anymore. Oh, it's just too much! I, I am going back to mother. *(Pause.)* I simply can't stand him any more.

TOMOKO: In what way?

TSUNEKO: Oh . . . in every possible way.

*Long silence.*

*Tomoko takes a long look at Tsuneko, who sits disconsolate, her face averted.*

TOMOKO: You quarrelled, didn't you?

TSUNEKO: No, it's nothing like that. *(Pause.)* I should have known better, I guess.

TOMOKO: You should have known better, you say. You mean something had been going on for some time?

TSUNEKO: No, but remember I used to tell you he has terrible manners.

TOMOKO: Is that the problem?

TSUNEKO: That's not all. Well, it is, actually, but it's more than just bad manners. I got entirely fed up with him.

TOMOKO: Men are all like that.

TSUNEKO: Remember, mother was annoyed at him for yawning in front of her one day? That sort of thing goes on constantly. It wouldn't bother me personally if he yawned in front of me. But he does things in front of other people, which embarrasses me no end.

TOMOKO: Such as?

TSUNEKO: I can't possibly list them all; there are just so many. . . . It was the same when we got on the train. Without a word he would stick his feet up on the seat and go soundly off to sleep. This, on the very first day of our trip.

TOMOKO: Without even talking to you?

TSUNEKO: Talk? I should say not. Why, one wonders what the point is in going on such a trip. People looked in our direction with funny expressions on their face, and with good reason, for there he was fast asleep with his mouth wide open, and not even a handkerchief over his face.

TOMOKO *(doing her best to keep from laughing)*: He was all tired out from the wedding and such.

TSUNEKO: Then, how about me, having to wear a tight sash that I seldom wear?

TOMOKO: You're different. You're a woman, after all.

TSUNEKO: So, you've already learned to say things like that.

*Tomoko is silent.*

TSUNEKO: And then when we got to the inn he would spend most of his time talking and joking with the maids. I tell you it's most unusual. When we were having dinner, for instance, I felt so embarrassed. But he was so crude! "You must be from Tokyo," he would say to the maid. "I thought so. The way you carry yourself, you look too stylish to be from the countryside." Just like that. The maid, she was real sharp. "Are you from Tokyo, too, sir?" she would say. Then he would scratch his head in an exaggerated manner and reply with a "That puts me in my place, I guess." Isn't that disgusting? Really.

TOMOKO: But you're being difficult, too, you know. That's the sort of thing men say . . . depending on the person he's talking to, that is.

TSUNEKO: Would your husband say things like that, too?

TOMOKO: Sure . . . Well, I don't know about *him*.

TSUNEKO: Oh, he surely wouldn't. But then something even worse happened. It was last night. I asked him what prefecture Kamagôri was in and he replied by asking me what prefecture I thought it was in. Do you know? I'm sure you don't. So I said Mie prefecture, you know, just at random. Then he smiled, and told me to draw a map of Japan and circle the area where I thought it would be in. I told him, no, I didn't want to do something that sounded too much like a high school test. Then he brought out a pad and pencil and insisted that I do it. He even suggested that I couldn't even draw a map of Japan. I was so annoyed that I told him that of course I could. Remember, we often used to draw maps. Well, I drew one like that, and you know what he said? I had no more than finished drawing the main island of Japan when he said, "What in the world is that, a cucumber?" *(She laughs and then dissolves into tears.)*

TOMOKO: What was it he said?

TSUNEKO: He asked if it was a cucumber. *(Starts crying again.)*

TOMOKO *(checks her feeling of annoyance and amusement)*: Why, how rude!

TSUNEKO: I don't know what made me want to marry him. He has nothing of what I would call "delicacy." *(Pause.)* Do you know how he washes his face in the morning? *(A sigh.)* And then when he gets into his suit jacket, he waves his arms in all directions. If he's going to be wearing Western clothes you'd think he'd at least learn how to get into them. Why, it's disgraceful!

TOMOKO: You are really bitter aren't you? But I don't think you are being fair. Don't you think he is a lot more refreshing than someone who is strangely affected?

TSUNEKO: But there's nothing refreshing about him at all. For one thing he only pretends to be unaffected. You do understand? He makes an affectation of being unaffected! That's why I get so irritated by his every act and every speech. I feel like saying, "Who do you think you are!"

TOMOKO: I wonder, though.

TSUNEKO: Take the wedding ceremony for example, the way he was trying to act so nonchalant, as if to say, "What a bother all this is," and yet actually he was nervous. Remember how he would often put on that look of innocence? That's his way of masking his embarrassment. Oh, am I to marry that woman? Oh, am I to take this cup of wine? Am I to go on a trip with her? That's the kind of face he puts on. In the first place, to be undecided about where one is going until he gets to a railroad station, that's just too much. Mother was terribly worried and asked him about it, but all he would say was "I really haven't decided, yet. Oh, I guess we'll take our chances and get off when the train stops. There really isn't any place that we are particularly anxious to see. Ha, ha, ha, ha, ha. . . . " That's the way he was. Mother and even my uncle looked the other way in disgust. But this is also a pose. He acts as if he didn't care, when he ought to know he's cutting a ridiculous figure.

TOMOKO: That I remember, too. Now that you mention it I did think he was odd.

TSUNEKO: And that's not all. Remember, everyone of you came to the railroad station to see us off and you came into our car and presented us with a bouquet of flowers. Do you remember what he said at that occasion?

TOMOKO *(firmly)*: Yes. "What am I suppose to do with this?" he asked, and then, "What a bother! One more thing to carry. They'll wilt in no time any way."

TSUNEKO: So, now you know what I mean. He says such tactless things deliberately to cover up his embarrassment. It would be all right if he said something clever, but he isn't that smart, and he ends up saying things that hurt other people's feelings.

TOMOKO: He is something of a problem, isn't he?

TSUNEKO: I feel like despising him, although perhaps I should feel sorry for him.

TOMOKO: That's putting it a bit too. . . .

TSUNEKO: No, I don't mind. I've made my decision.

TOMOKO: Decision?

TSUNEKO: Yes. I'm leaving him.

*Long silence.*

TOMOKO: Wait, now, you shouldn't give up that easily. *(Pause)*: Men, you know, are like. . . .

TSUNEKO: Thank you, I have had enough of your preaching on that subject. What are men like? Who decided that men are such and so? Had I known that you also accepted such views I wouldn't have discussed this matter with you at all.

TOMOKO: Don't say that. Let's think about this some more. Your marriage may not have turned out the way you imagined. But if what I just heard is all that is the matter I would hardly consider the situation to be as critical as you seem to believe. In the first place his behavior is no proof that he doesn't love you.

TSUNEKO: So what? Whether one is loved or not is a secondary question.

TOMOKO: What?

TSUNEKO: The first question is whether he is the sort of person whose love for you would make you feel happy.

TOMOKO: But then you knew that. . . .

TSUNEKO: From the very beginning, I suppose is what you meant to say. Yes, I did, as a matter of fact, but what if I had been wrong? Or even if I hadn't been, what if I had made the wrong wish? You are happy and that is why you simply do not appreciate my problems. *(Sobs.)*

*Silence.*

TOMOKO *(sternly)*: What are you talking about? I hate to be the one to say this, but no one is more concerned about you than I. Surely you came here and nowhere else to talk this thing over because you knew this to be the case. I am quite willing to do all I can. Let's have it out. It doesn't do any good to get angry the way you do.

TSUNEKO: Sis, I don't want to leave things like this. There is one thing that I haven't told you about, but since you put it that way I will tell you everything. I know you'll be astonished. This is one thing that even I simply cannot take.

TOMOKO: Just a minute now. Calm yourself. There are certain things that once done can never be undone. I don't want you to think that just because you've told me about it I would tell it to someone else. But I don't want you to do anything that would injure your own pride. It may be unreasonable for me to ask you to be calm at this moment. But at least I have to stay calm, don't you think? For your sake. So get a hold on yourself and just tell me the facts without getting emotional about it, that is, if you are sure that you want to mention it to me.

*Long silence.*

TSUNEKO: You make it hard for me to go on.

TOMOKO: Maybe you should keep it to yourself, then.

TSUNEKO: But if I do I won't be able to make you understand how I feel. Besides, I don't care if I do tell you. There just is no way of finding a happy solution. You see. . . .

TOMOKO *(getting to her feet)*: I'll be back in a minute. Aren't you hungry?

TSUNEKO: No.

TOMOKO: But still. You'll have to take potluck.

TSUNEKO: Don't bother, really. I am going straight back to Mother's.

TOMOKO: To Mother's? Why? In any case, I want to talk to you some more. All right? *(Leaves the room.)*

*Long interval.*

HOUSEKEEPER *(brings in some tea)*: How do you do.

*Tsuneko nods in return.*

HOUSEKEEPER: I didn't know you were here. *(Serves her a cup of tea)*: Have you returned already?

TSUNEKO: Yes.

*Exit Housekeeper.*

YUZURU *(entering)*: Well, hello. You back already? That was a quick trip.

TSUNEKO *(embarrassed)*: I became lonely for Tokyo.

YUZURU: Well, I guess even honeymoons are gradually getting to be no more than form. It is as though one were observing this practice only because others observe it, and it probably holds no more appeal. But then maybe that's something one feels in retrospect, and that actually one is rather carried away by the whole thing while one is going through with it.

TOMOKO *(entering)*: What are you going on about? Listen. . . . *She whispers something in his ear.*

YUZURU *(in a cheerful vein)*: Oh, is that so. Well, if you will excuse me. Do make yourself at home. *(Getting to his feet)*: She's joining us for supper, though, isn't she?

TOMOKO: Of course.

TSUNEKO: You don't have to go, Yuzuru. Sis, I don't mind having

Yuzuru stay here. I would just as soon have it that way. I would like
to have him listen to me and give me his advice.

TOMOKO: If that's the way you feel. . . . I don't care one way or
another. *(She looks at one and then the other.)* Well, let's have him
stay, then. After all, if worse comes to worst we will need his
advice.

YUZURU *(feigning calmness)*: What is the matter, anyway? So formal. . .
. *(He sits down.)*

TOMOKO: How about first telling him the gist of what happened?

*Tsuneko is silent.*

TOMOKO: I guess it is a bit hard to put it in a few words. How shall we
put it?

YUZURU: Just give me a simple account. Has anything gone wrong?

TOMOKO *(her eyes on Tsuneko)*: I wouldn't put it quite that way, but. . .
. Well, I might as well start off. You don't mind, do you? It's that
marriage! *(Pause.)* According to Tsuneko it evidently isn't working
out well. I guess it is a case of incompatibility rather than any one
particular thing that happened. Evidently he hasn't the slightest
understanding for the way a young woman might feel.

YUZURU: Well, but look. . . .

TOMOKO: Yes, I mentioned that to Tsuneko also, a moment ago. But,
evidently it never occurred to her that things would be that bad.
Mother, for one, had been worried about it, and I had also gently
called Tsuneko's attention to it. But then when it gets to be a question of degree, well, maybe it was a case of poor judgment. I know
it's in front of Tsuneko, but there are circumstances in which one can
be one-sided in one's interpretations. I don't for a minute want to put
the sole blame on Tsuneko, but. . . . I also feel a certain amount of
responsibility in this matter.

TSUNEKO: You shouldn't feel that way at all. You didn't. . . .

TOMOKO: Let me finish. So, Tsuneko wants to rethink her whole future
although it may seem indecent to be talking this way now.

YUZURU: How about being more specific?

TSUNEKO: Well. . . . *(She looks into her sister's face.)*

TOMOKO: Evidently it's quite involved. I wonder where would be the
best place to start. Tsuneko, what was the one thing that repelled you
the most? The one thing you felt you could least put up with?

TSUNEKO: That was what I was about to tell you a while ago. I will tell
it, because otherwise you wouldn't understand. *(Pause.)* It was last
night. *(Pause.)* By coincidence I met a person at the inn whom he
claimed to be an old friend. I had never heard of him before. And he

came to our room during the evening and the two men started to drink. That was all right, except that both of them got drunk and boisterous. I thought this was too much, so I suggested that the people in the next room might be bothered by the noise. Then he shouted, "Mind your own business!" and both of them went out and didn't return for hours. I waited up for him all night and when he came back . . . it was already getting light outside . . . he had a funny look on his face and snickered as he looked at me.

*Long silence.*

*Tomoko, her eyes brimming with tears, is looking at her husband.*

TSUNEKO: Even so for a while I said nothing, and then I just gently proposed that we return to Tokyo. Then he asked if I was angry. "No," I said, "I just want to return to Tokyo, and if you'd rather, I will go alone."

*Silence.*

TSUNEKO: "If you want to go back, let's go back. But there's no reason to get upset over what happened last night. I had to tag along," he said, as if it was the most natural thing to do. And here I was deeply resolved that this was one time I would not forgive him no matter how much he apologized. I was so outraged that I asked him bluntly if he didn't feel ashamed in my presence. *(Pause.)* Then he said, "I have done nothing for which I should feel ashamed, and if you want to be suspicious that's your business!" So I said, "It isn't a question of being suspicious. Your behavior is not only a mark of your contempt for me, but for your own self as well." I didn't quite put it in such complicated terms, but I meant to express the idea. Could be that I had no voice by then. *(Pause.)* My heart was ready to burst.

*Long pause.*

TOMOKO: Is that all? Have you said all you want to say?

*Tsuneko nods.*

TOMOKO *(turning to her husband)*: What do you think about this?

YUZURU: I would say he is a little rude.

TOMOKO: What do you mean "a little"! What did he do then?

TSUNEKO: Nothing. From that point on he didn't say a word. Both of us said absolutely nothing to each other until we arrived in Tokyo Station. I just said I was going to stop off to see Mother and we parted, and that was it.

TOMOKO: Then he doesn't know that you came here, I suppose.

TSUNEKO: Oh, he must know that I would.

YUZURU: But look Tsune, men, you know, are. . . .

TOMOKO: We've had enough of that sort of sermon.

YUZURU: How come?

TOMOKO: Tsuneko said that to me earlier. Besides after an experience like that, one wouldn't be able to accept this "Men, you know" stuff. *(Pause.)* But anyway let's hear what you have to suggest.

YUZURU *(stiffening)*: You make it hard for me. Well, I have no intention of defending men as such. But, you must understand that problems like this should be approached a little more from the angle of the motive. One cannot be overly critical purely by observing surface facts.

TOMOKO: But after all. . . .

YUZURU: Just wait. Now let me try offering an explanation for him. *(Pause.)* The fact of the matter is that he was greeted by this friend of his with "A lot of fun, I bet," and was feeling a little embarrassed. He felt that this friend, being the kind that he was, was very likely to spread a story to the effect that he stuck close to his bride all the time and hardly talked to this friend. In fact he even thought that this friend would make some nasty remarks about how anxious he was at night to be left alone with his bride. This is putting it a bit crudely. Now he wasn't going to let this fellow get away with that. He was going to show him that he was above that sort of stuff, and one way of doing it was to have a leisurely dinner with him, have some drinks, and show him that his bride wasn't his sole interest.

*Tsuneko tries to say something.*

YUZURU: Let me finish. So trusting in his wife and taking advantage of his wife's trust in him he started planning things out. But once the plans started unfolding he noticed his wife's displeasure. So then he bawled her out, although in his heart he was full of remorse. "That a boy!" flashed in this friend's eyes, and he, while looking triumphant, tried to show his regret to his bride, but she wouldn't get it at all.

TOMOKO: Don't joke any more.

YUZURU: I am not joking at all. Tsune, you don't think I am trying to be funny, do you? You mustn't judge a thing from the way it sounds. This is not something that can be solved by arguing. All that is needed here is to understand his feeling at the time. Isn't that so, Tsune?

*Tsuneko remains silent, her eyes on the floor.*

YUZURU: So he said to himself, "If I don't act fast I might make that one fatal slip that could destroy the very effect of my triumph. The safest course is to retire from the scene. I can tell her about it later, and if I explained it to her carefully she would surely understand, and even if I didn't explain anything she should be able to understand what I was

up to if she'd use her head. After all she is a very intelligent girl."
So he feigned being hopelessly drunk and left his wife's presence.
Now all should have been well by then, but his friend was one of
those pests who twitted him with remarks like, "Going back already?
Feeling that lonely?" So, having gone this far, he decided to play the
game to the bitter end. The next morning he finally managed to mol-
lify his friend and flew back to his wife's side with a feeling of
immense relief. And as he expected, he found his wife all alone waiting for him with swollen eyes. Now if he had been a Westerner he
would have searched for tender and loving words: "Oh, my loving
wife, my darling, how amazed you must have been, how wretched
you must have felt, how provoked you must be. To prove that I
cherish you, et cetera, et cetera" But Japanese men express all this by
. . . what was it that he did? Oh, yes, by snickering. Now if she had
been a Western girl she would threaten her husband with words like:
"You sure made me feel wretched. Don't you ever do that again. If
you do there's no telling whom I might run off with." But a Japanese
woman knows how to handle situations like this and with her chin
buried deep in the collar of her dress she would maintain a stolid
silence with her eyes fixed on the edging of the *tatami* floor. What a
deep effect it has of making the husband feel ashamed of himself, and
even if she were to say something at all, it would be a very indirect
statement like "Let's go back to Tokyo."

TOMOKO: My you are talkative today, aren't you? How about bringing it
to an end? We get the general idea. We don't have to hear the rest
do we, Tsune? It's very obvious.

*Tsuneko nods.*

YUZURU: Exactly how did you understand it? If I'm cut off at this point
I know that what I have said so far would sound like sarcasm. But I
don't mean it that way. Now up to this point, you see, everything is
all right. There is no problem. The situation got involved after this
point. In other words, from the point where he said, "Are you
angry?" and you said, "No." But even this, according to my inter-
pretation, at any rate, is all a matter of a temporary discrepancy in
each other's feelings.

TOMOKO *(in a very serious tone)*: Do you really believe what you have
just said?

YUZURU: Now, what do you mean by that? All I did was to offer an
opinion that seemed the most sensible on the basis of the information
you, I mean Tsuneko, presented. So if Tsuneko decides, after due
consideration of the circumstances and whatever else, that what I had

said must have been the case, then there is really nothing to get too concerned about. The only remaining problem in that case is how to go about effecting a reconciliation . . . a very mundane problem, I might say.

TOMOKO: I am not asking you about that, at all. Tsune, what do you think?

TSUNEKO *(with much reserve)*: May I be allowed to speak out frankly?

TOMOKO: Why, of course. *(She glances in the direction of her husband.)*

YUZURU: You don't need to stand on ceremony with me. Go right ahead. I feel hungry though.

TOMOKO: The meal is all ready, but let's talk until we come to a good breaking point. Wouldn't that be better?

YUZURU: Fine. Tsuneko, what is your opinion?

TSUNEKO: What you said may be a perfectly good excuse . . . for a man. But for a woman, well, this sounds a bit too grandiose, doesn't it? Let's just say that I for one am not in the least bit impressed by such an explanation. Such an attitude in a man, one in which he would ignore a woman and think nothing of it, is something that I cannot possibly respect.

TOMOKO: I would certainly agree with that.

TSUNEKO: So I am going to take a stand.

YUZURU: That you can do later. I suppose you feel that his behavior is inexcusable regardless of his reasons.

TSUNEKO: It isn't a question of excusing. It's a question of the difference between us in our attitude toward life.

TOMOKO: I entirely agree with you.

TSUNEKO: It isn't just in this one incident that the difference is apparent. I find it in everything he does, and I just can't stand it.

YUZURU: Since when did you begin to feel that way?

TSUNEKO: Since the day we were married.

YUZURU: All of a sudden?

TSUNEKO: It suddenly became noticeable.

TOMOKO: Don't you think that the change is due, not so much to any sudden change in his attitude, as a feeling in you that with marriage you had come to a turning point in your life? Things like that happen, you know. When you start thinking that from this moment you are embarking on a new life with this person, you begin to see him in a new light. It is then that the little considerations which the man shows you as your husband begin to affect you in every way, to produce elation or dejection. From my own experience. . . . *(As she says this she turns and gently smiles to her husband.)*

*Yuzuru nods frequently in obvious agreement. He has a very serious look on his face.*

TSUNEKO: I suppose that's part of it.

YUZURU: But that cuts both ways. The same thing could be true for men. Of course men probably aren't as preoccupied with such things as women. But there are many, many instances in which, after you have been married, you come to know that certain things turn out as you had anticipated, while others do not.

TOMOKO *(a little embarrassed)*: A disenchantment, in other words. But then being prudent, a woman will. . . .

YUZURU: I wonder. . . .

TOMOKO: At least make an effort to adapt herself to her husband's way of life.

YUZURU: Sure, on the surface at least.

TOMOKO: More than that. They sacrifice a lot to do this.

YUZURU: What sort of sacrifice?

TOMOKO: If she does not share her husband's tastes she would even sacrifice her own taste for the sake of her husband.

YUZURU: You must be thinking of music.

TOMOKO: But that's not all.

YUZURU: What else do you have in mind? Oh, that! Is that what you have in mind? *(He looks up at the ceiling sardonically as if he wanted to laugh.)*

TOMOKO: What do you mean? What could you be referring to?

YUZURU: What are you asking for!

TOMOKO *(beginning to laugh)*: Well, that's a long time ago. In any case you have no right to say such things to me. Don't say such queer things in front of Tsuneko.

TSUNEKO: Sis. . . .

TOMOKO: Oh, that's all right. He's always like that; it doesn't matter in whose presence.

YUZURU *(laughing)*: Maybe I'm just like Tsuneko's husband then?

TSUNEKO: Of course not. You are a fine person. In the first place you took some eighty pictures of your bride on your honeymoon.

YUZURU: My, you have a good memory! Didn't your husband take any?

TSUNEKO: He doesn't have such fancy things like cameras in the first place. Not even a walking cane.

TOMOKO: What, he doesn't carry a walking cane? What does he carry when he walks? An umbrella?

TSUNEKO: That and a briefcase. He walks with a huge briefcase. Refuses to let a redcap carry it for him. Says that he can carry it for himself.

YUZURU: He's physically strong, then.

TSUNEKO *(vaguely)*:   Yes.   He even carries luggage for other people when getting off the train.

TOMOKO: It shows he is quite thoughtful on such matters.

TSUNEKO: And yet he won't even offer me a hand when I get on and off a train.   He just goes right on ahead by himself.

TOMOKO *(to her husband)*:   Evidently slept all the way from Tokyo Station.

YUZURU: Who?

TOMOKO: That person.   Evidently snored away, paying no attention to Tsuneko, with his mouth hanging open.

YUZURU: Something is wrong with his nose, maybe.

TOMOKO: Something is wrong with his manners.   Even at the inn he evidently did things that terribly embarrassed her.   He seems to think nothing of joking with the waitress in front of her.   Apparently he has terrible manners in eating.   Evidently he has nothing of the gentleman in him.   *(She looks straight at her husband.)*

YUZURU: So what?   *(Avoids meeting his wife's eyes.)*   That is nothing to get so upset about.

TOMOKO: What she dislikes in him most of all apparently is the way he deliberately puts on an expression of disinterest.   No matter how beautiful the scenery, he would let it pass without comment.   When he eats you can practically guarantee that he would look as if the food tasted terrible, and if you say you are going to buy some presents he would look displeased, on the grounds that they will make more baggage.   Evidently very discouraging.

*Yuzuru chuckles to himself, as he suspects that Tomoko is really talking about him.*

TOMOKO: Besides, he evidently is unkempt.   He doesn't comb his hair after his bath *(glances at her husband's uncombed hair)*, leaves his nails untrimmed *(Yuzuru steals a glance at his nails)*; you suggest a walk and he says, "You can see the ocean from here lying down.   All you get out of a walk is fatigue!"   Apparently he's like this in everything.

*Yuzuru now has a strong suspicion that Tomoko is talking about him and looks in the direction of Tsuneko as if to say, "Well, well, I wonder who she's talking about now?"*

*While mystified by her sister's amazing faculty of imagination, Tsuneko cannot conceal that she is also rather impressed by it.*

TOMOKO *(becoming more and more eloquent)*:   And yet in spite of it all he tries to show off at such silly occasions. He asks what prefecture a certain county is in, and thinking that anybody could tell she apparently said nothing. Then he got all puffed up and like a school teacher ordered her to draw a map of Japan and circle the area where it was located. He became very insistent, because he thought she didn't know, so she says she went ahead and drew a map of Japan. She had drawn only the main island when he turned to her and said, "What's that, an egg-plant?"

TSUNEKO: No, Sis, a cucumber.

YUZURU: I see. *(He laughs.)*

TOMOKO: Isn't he rude? *(Pause.)* How could one get into the mood of being newlyweds? It's so unromantic! To have to start out a new life this way is too bad, don't you think?

YUZURU: So, what is your opinion? Do you agree with Tsuneko? *(Pause.)* I don't think there is a simple solution. *(Pause.)* What would you do, if it happened to you?

TOMOKO: Tsuneko and I are different. I can't judge it on the basis of my situation. Tsuneko's ideals are higher than mine.

TSUNEKO: That is not true. But perhaps I shouldn't have come to you for advice on such matters. As a matter of fact, I don't feel in the least bit in doubt as to what action I should take, but I thought I would tell you about it first, because I was sure that if I waited until it was all over you would ask me why I hadn't mentioned this to you before. At any rate what you had to say was very informative.

TOMOKO: You still intend to be separated from him then?

TSUNEKO: Yes.

YUZURU: But Tsuneko, it would be a mistake to think that a greater happiness is in store for you. I think you need to keep in mind the possibility that your next marriage, assuming that you get married again, may be an even less fortunate one. You may say then that you won't get mixed up in that kind of marriage. But your experience has shown that marriage is something that you can't be certain of until you've taken the step. Wouldn't you agree? Of course, if you are determined to seek out your own destiny in search of that elusive happiness that's something else again. If you find meaning in a kind of life in which you would doggedly search for your goal in the face of repeated reverses, even to lie exhausted without achieving your objective, that, too, is something else entirely. You can't keep moving from one man to the next until you find the ideal husband. Are you really sure that you will ever meet the man with whom you will be satisfied? I don't think so. If you don't, then what? This is also something you should give some thought to. A divorce presents a rather complicated problem. *(Pause.)* It would have to be in the form of a divorce, wouldn't it? For you're married. . . .

TOMOKO: I guess so, although it's been only a week or so. . . .

YUZURU: Of course, having lived together only a short time you would naturally have that much less to lose. But then you have lost the most important thing.

*Tomoko looks sorrowfully in the direction of Tsuneko.*

YUZURU: This is a very conventional argument, I know, but in terms of the normal concept of virtue you have lost your right to select a husband as a virgin. And even if you were to marry a second time under the most ideal conditions the new husband-wife relationship cannot be a pure one. There is sure to be something that will come between you, and the more you love each other the more it becomes pronounced. Of course it is possible to build a beautiful relationship through the efforts of both parties. But I think one can safely say that it would be an exceptional case.

TSUNEKO: I don't have any particular desire to get married again, nor do I think that I will be able to begin a happy life tomorrow if I were to be separated from him today. But I can't help but feel that it would be senseless to live with a person like him when I find him so distasteful. I wouldn't mind being punished in some other way for having unwisely chosen such a husband. For instance, I think I would be able to accept the verdict of having to be spinster the rest of my life. And if I'm willing to take such a step I think I would be far more true to myself if I just decided to be separated.

YUZURU: What good would it do to be true only to yourself?

TOMOKO: That's right. You shouldn't be thinking only of yourself.

TSUNEKO: Then whom am I supposed to think about.

TOMOKO: Everyone involved. In the first place, Mother. Imagine how worried she will be.

YUZURU: Before we get to that let's think about your husband. Do you realize that you may be putting your husband into a hopeless position? What will you do then? Don't you care what happens to him?

TSUNEKO: You don't seem to realize that he has no concern for me. In fact he trampled upon our happiness with complete impunity. Why, he has done nothing to indicate that there is any hope for a happy life together. Since that is the case don't you think it would be useless for me alone to strive to do this or that?

YUZURU: How do you know that it would be useless after only a week or so?

TSUNEKO *(tearfully)*: You are determined, aren't you, to persuade me into a life of perseverances, to make me only do something that two people should be working together at. Sis, I refuse to do that. *(Wipes her tears.)*

*Silence.*

TSUNEKO: It is one thing if he has the will, but not the strength. I would certainly be willing to work at it alone. But having the strength if he refuses to make the effort . . . if he has no intention, then I simply cannot bring myself to trying it alone. Nor am I interested. I won't, I won't, if it means death I still won't. *(Weeps silently.)*

TOMOKO *(moved to tears herself, but her voice still cheerful)*: Come on, pull yourself together. This is no time to be crying. Oh, dear, what to do? Surely he isn't deliberately trying to make you unhappy. It could be that he does something that seems the most natural thing for him to do, and yet it upsets you. And probably any woman would find it upsetting. But in your case you say it is more than just upsetting. It even casts a dark shadow on your whole life. I know such things can happen. But then if he isn't doing these things out of malice, don't you think that over a long time you could make him change his ways?

TSUNEKO: No, it's part of his character.

TOMOKO: I guess you're right. It's not the same as being just rude.

YUZURU: I think it's a case of degree. Men have deficiencies of that sort when viewed by women. Talk about personality and so forth. It's just a matter of habit. I don't want to say anything irresponsible here, but if you are determined not to allow a man to be selfish, you should discard your position of being subordinate to men. And in order to love each other in the true sense of the word you should demonstrate that you are entirely a man's equal in ability.

TSUNEKO: By equal ability you mean I should become economically independent, I suppose.

YUZURU: Not necessarily economically. For example, I become a school teacher. *(Glancing toward his wife)*: *This girl* becomes a clerk in a store. *(Tomoko and Tsuneko look at each other.)*

TOMOKO *(looking disgusted)*: What do you mean *this girl*?

YUZURU: It's a way of indicating an intimate relationship. But such an arrangement alone will not make a woman independent. Whenever something comes up *this girl* comes to me for advice: "What shall we do?"

TOMOKO: I do not!

YUZURU: You do, too.  You can't possibly call this equality of ability, can you now?

TOMOKO: All one needs is for both parties to consult each other on all matters.

YUZURU: "What shall we do?"

TOMOKO: That's enough, thank you.

YUZURU: Boy, what a messed up situation!  Anyway, Tsuneko, why don't you go back to your husband today.  And ask nonchalantly to be taken to the theatre.  Tell him that we'll go along, too.

TOMOKO *(airily)*:  That's a wonderful idea.  *(Earnestly)*:  Why don't you?

*Tsuneko cannot put herself into the mood.  Her eyes are on some distant object.*

YUZURU *(getting to his feet slowly)*:  I'm going to go comb my hair before supper, and trim my nails while I'm at it.  After all, I am having the pleasure of Madame Tsuneko Saitô's company for dinner.

TSUNEKO *(throws a quick glance at Tomoko and starts to smile, and then with an air of seriousness)*:  Sis, I am going to ask you to excuse me today.  It's kind of you, but I just don't feel up to it.

TOMOKO: Excuse you to go where?

TSUNEKO *(in a low voice)*:  To Mother's.

TOMOKO *(also in a low voice)*:  You are still determined, then?

*Long silence.*

TSUNEKO: Well, I had better be going.  Yuzuru, I'm sorry to have troubled you with my silly problems.

YUZURU: Think it over.  *(To his wife)*:  How about seeing her off, then.

TOMOKO: Yes.  But Tsuneko, going there now would only. . . .

TSUNEKO: That's all right.  Don't worry about me.  Good-bye.  I'll come over again very soon, maybe tomorrow.

TOMOKO: Well, if that's how you feel.  But wait a second.  I'll walk a little ways with you.

TSUNEKO: No, really you don't have to.  I am all right.  *(As they get to their feet there is a sudden cloudburst.  All three silently look out through the window.  Tsuneko takes a deep breath.)*

TOMOKO: What wretched weather it has turned into.

YUZURU: It will clear soon enough.  Why don't you sit down and wait a while.

*Long silence.*
*Curtain.*

# A DIARY OF FALLEN LEAVES

(1927)

translated by

David G. Goodman
and
J. Thomas Rimer

*Characters:*
    Dowager
    Osamu, her grandson
    Henriette, her granddaughter
    Hiroshi, Henriette's friend
    Tsuru, a maid
    Kazue, Dowager's daughter and Osamu's mother
    Doctor

*Time:*
    An autumn afternoon.

*Place:*
    A wooded suburb of Tokyo.

## ACT ONE

*Two chairs are aligned on a villa patio. In one sits the Dowager; her grandson Osamu reclines in the other. They seem completely at ease, as if they regularly assume this posture. They are reading quietly.*

*Dowager is dressed casually in pure Japanese style, except for the fur stole thrown over her shoulders, which does not appear particularly incongruous.*

*The young man wears a jaunty walking outfit; his head is uncovered.*

OSAMU *(making no attempt to catch the book that is slipping from his fingers)*: How about a little walk?

DOWAGER *(without taking her eyes from her book)*: I only have two or three pages to go.

*Osamu gets up and waits in silence for her to finish reading. She shows no sign of doing so, however, so he sits down again.*

DOWAGER *(without looking up)*: Please do sit still!

OSAMU *(distractedly)*: I am sitting still.

*A long silence.*

OSAMU *(as if speaking to himself)*: I guess even old people become preoccupied.

*Dowager does not react.*

OSAMU: Of course, I mean lost in thought. That is, you wouldn't become so preoccupied as to lose track of what's going on around you. You could pay attention if you wanted to. The fact that you don't simply means that you don't choose to. It just doesn't make much difference to you whether you pay attention or not. You see what I mean? In other words. . . .

DOWAGER *(her eyes on her book)*: Osamu, must you ramble on so?

OSAMU *(smiling but determined)*: Grandmother, for you the best of all possible worlds would be if everyone went around like that with their backs bent, peering through bifocals, reading some religious tract.

DOWAGER: So what if it were? What a bother you are! *(She thrusts her book under the young man's nose.)* Does this look like a religious tract?

OSAMU *(taken aback)*: Anatole France, *La Vie en Fleur*.[1] You'd better be careful. A writer like that can get you into a lot of trouble.

DOWAGER: Don't be ridiculous. Now get ready to go. *(She begins to get up.)*

OSAMU *(stopping her)*: Before we do, Grandmother, there's something I'd like to discuss. *(Pause.)* You don't mind if we talk about it here, do you?

*Dowager looks at him quizzically.*

OSAMU: Please. . . . *(He helps her into her chair again.)* This is hard . . . . I mean. . . .

DOWAGER: Osamu, do get to the point, will you!

OSAMU: All right, all right. But don't look at me that way. Please?

DOWAGER: What way? You can avert your eyes if you're uncomfortable. Now what do you want from me?

OSAMU: Then you already know?

DOWAGER: Know what? Just tell me what's on your mind.

*Pause.*

OSAMU: Grandmother, what kind of marriage do you intend to arrange for Henriette?

DOWAGER: It isn't up to me to arrange her marriage. She has a perfectly splendid father who can manage all that.

OSAMU: But that perfectly splendid father of hers is forever traveling abroad, and ever since her mother died, you, being her grandmother, have taken charge of her affairs. So naturally, when the question of marriage comes up, your approval. . . .

DOWAGER: Now just a moment. It's true that I've borne a certain responsibility for Henriette's upbringing, but that's all. She's been educated to make her own decisions.

OSAMU: Of course she has.

DOWAGER: How insufferably rude you are! Look at you, you can hardly tell your right hand from your left. And that ridiculous law you're studying, what do you expect to come of that? Henriette's highly intelligent and fully capable of looking out for herself.

---

[1]Kishida quotes the original French text of *La Vie en Fleur* (1922), untranslated, in the dialogue that follows. For the convenience of the reader, I have appended an English translation of the corresponding passages. The translation is taken from *The Bloom of Life*, tr. J. Lewis May (New York:

OSAMU: Too good for me, is that it? Tell me, then, Grandmother, what
sort of man do you like?

DOWAGER: Do I like?

OSAMU *(flustered)*: I mean setting aside the problem of age.

DOWAGER: What has age got to do with it? That's the trouble with you.
Young or old, women are women. Laugh at me, will you? Well,
I've got a thing or two to say about men like you. In the first place,
you're vain. . . . *(She pretends to be cross.)*

OSAMU *(changing the subject)*: Grandmother, there are some leaves
caught in your hair.

*Dowager removes the leaves without ceremony.*

OSAMU: How old were you when you got married, Grandmother?

DOWAGER: Why do you ask?

OSAMU: Just curious.

DOWAGER: Actually, I was quite young. It was the spring of my
eighteenth year. I was Henriette's age and had just graduated from
high school. You remember the Pariani family? Well, I was studying
Italian with Origa, their mother.

OSAMU: You were waiting for Grandfather to come for you from Rome,
is that it? What about Grandfather?

DOWAGER: You mean his age? Well, he wasn't a youngster like you,
that's for certain. He already had a moustache and was a very distinguished gentleman.

OSAMU: I like the part about his being distinguished. That's a nice
touch. And you, Grandmother, were no doubt a graceful beauty.

DOWAGER: It goes without saying! I wasn't as tall as your mother, but I
wasn't as petite as Henriette either.

OSAMU: Of course. It goes without saying. And you were good at
horseback riding and the broad jump too, I expect.

DOWAGER *(laughing)*: As a matter of fact, no.

OSAMU: You know, Grandmother, I was looking through Mother's things
the other day, and I found a photograph of you and Grandfather taken
when you were in Paris. You're wearing a frayed-looking black cape
over your shoulders. I think it must have been at the Luxembourg.
There's a statue of someone or other in the background. You're feed-
ing the pigeons with your hands spread like this. I was so impressed,
all I could do was sit down with my mouth ajar and stare.

Dodd, Mead and Company, 1923), pp. 203-206. D.G.G.

DOWAGER: I don't remember a photograph like that. What's Grandfather doing in it?

OSAMU: Nothing much, just holding his walking stick parallel to the ground with both hands, as if it were a barbell or something. And he's gazing at you, captivated by your beautiful, young profile.

DOWAGER: Oh, do stop!

OSAMU: You have to give him credit for that moustache, though.

DOWAGER: His moustache?

OSAMU: Absolutely.

DOWAGER: You know, I haven't looked at those photographs in ages. I must have some among my things as well. Oh, now I remember when that was taken!

*A long silence.*

OSAMU: They all died young, didn't they? Grandfather, my father, and Henriette's mother, too.

DOWAGER: Yes. Quite young. Yvonne wasn't even thirty.

OSAMU: I have a feeling I'll die young myself. Somehow I made it through this most recent illness, but. . . .

DOWAGER: That's the trouble with you: you're always putting yourself down.

OSAMU: I am not! As a matter of fact, I invited Henriette to play tennis with me today, but Mr. Judo Expert had to butt in and say I wasn't up to it; and Henriette just went along with him. She wouldn't even give me a second glance.

DOWAGER: *Tu es bête!*

*A long silence.*

DOWAGER: Aren't you cold? You're not wearing a coat. The wind's chilly today.

OSAMU: A month passes so quickly! *(Pause.)* When I arrived, the leaves on the poplars weren't nearly so yellow. But you'd never know I'd been sick to look at me, would you?

DOWAGER: No, but you'd better take it easy for the next year or so. You wouldn't want to have a relapse.

OSAMU *(his expression darkening suddenly)*: Let's forget the beach. I'd rather stay here.

*Pause.*

DOWAGER: If it only weren't so cold. This place just wasn't made for winter living.

OSAMU: In any case, it's no place for me, is it?

DOWAGER: Why do you say that?

OSAMU: Why? Of all people, Grandmother, you should know.

DOWAGER: Now don't start up again. Take your leave like a man. I know I'm partly to blame. I should have understood your feelings and tried to intervene on your behalf earlier. But it's too late now. Now it's up to you. Happiness is yours . . .

OSAMU: For the taking? But I'm as happy now as I've ever been. It's true. Henriette still enjoys being alone with me occasionally. And every morning, the breakfast table is set for just the two of us. Everyone knows you prefer to sleep in.

DOWAGER: *Pauvre garçon!*

OSAMU: Here the sun is about to set, and soon the three of us will be together again. See, just the thought makes me happy!

DOWAGER *(laying her hand on his shoulder)*: If you feel so well, then there's no need to cry. Come along, let's take a stroll.

*Osamu is silent.*

DOWAGER: On your feet now.

*Henriette enters. She is young, dressed in tennis togs, and swings a tennis racquet.*

HENRIETTE: I'm so thirsty!

DOWAGER: Are you done so soon?

HENRIETTE: Soon? It's so dark you can hardly see the ball!

DOWAGER: No, I suppose not.

HENRIETTE: But it's not time for dinner yet, is it? Osamu, what's wrong?

DOWAGER: Chateaubriand has made him cry.

HENRIETTE: You mean he's crying over a novel? How silly!

DOWAGER: You leave Osamu alone. What about Hiroshi?

HENRIETTE: Well, he was on his way to say good-bye to you, and then he saw this persimmon tree--you know the one--and he insisted we pick some. I told him I would ask your permission and that he should wait for me.

DOWAGER: But they're not ripe yet, are they?

HENRIETTE: They're red on the outside. You don't mind if we pick them, do you?

DOWAGER: I suppose not, but be careful.

HENRIETTE: We will. *(She starts to go.)*

OSAMU *(getting up)*: I'll go too. *(He follows her.)*

DOWAGER: Tell Tsuru to find you a bamboo pole.

OSAMU: That's a good idea! *(He runs off toward the rear.)*

DOWAGER *(reproving)*: Don't run!

*As Osamu exits, Hiroshi enters.*

HENRIETTE: Hiroshi!

HIROSHI:  It's getting late; I'd better be going.  I don't want to get scolded again.

HENRIETTE *(disappointed)*:  But you said!

HIROSHI:  The persimmons will still be there tomorrow.

HENRIETTE:  I suppose so, but you're the one who. . . .

HIROSHI *(laughing her off cheerfully, to Dowager)*:  I'll be going, then.  *(He doffs his hat and exits at a run.)*

DOWAGER:  Regards to your family!

*Once Hiroshi is gone, Osamu returns with the bamboo pole.*

HENRIETTE *(trying to snatch the pole)*:  Here, let me have it!

OSAMU:  It's too heavy for you.

HENRIETTE:  I want to do it!

DOWAGER:  Henriette!

HENRIETTE *(glancing sidelong at her grandmother, she thrusts the pole back toward Osamu)*:  But I get to pick some too.

*Osamu and Henriette exit together.*

*After watching the two of them exit, Dowager once again begins turning the pages of her book.*

*A long silence.*

HENRIETTE'S VOICE:  That one's good.  No, more this way.  Yes, there!  Don't you see it, it's the red one!  What's wrong with you, are you blind?

*Occasionally Henriette's voice seems to distract Dowager, but her eyes quickly return to the page.  She begins reading aloud.*

DOWAGER:  *"J'étais loin d'être un beau garçon et le pis est que je manquais de hardiesse. Cela me nuisait auprès des femmes."*[2]

HENRIETTE'S VOICE:  Don't poke them so hard.  You'll bruise them.  Here, let me try.  *(Pause.)*  Don't worry! Just watch me.

DOWAGER *(reading aloud)*:  *"Car j'estimais que le plus grand péché d'une femme est de n'être pas belle."*[3]

HENRIETTE'S VOICE:  Now what are you doing?  Don't climb the tree, you'll get hurt!

*Dowager reacts slightly to these words, but immediately returns to her reading.*

DOWAGER:  *"Je remarquais que dans le monde, beaucoup de jeunes gens, qui ne me valaient pas, plaisaient et réussissaient mieux que*

---

[2]"I was not at all a good-looking youth and, what was still more unfortunate, I

*moi.* "[4]

HENRIETTE'S VOICE: That branch is full of ripe ones.  Yes, that's it, the one you're on now

DOWAGER: *"J'ai toujours cru que la seule chose raisonnable est de chercher le plaisir.*"[5]

HENRIETTE'S VOICE *(shouting to be heard)*: Grandmother.  Grandmother!  Osamu has climbed all the way up to the top of the tree.

*Dowager looks up, knits her brow slightly, but immediately returns to her book.*

DOWAGER: *"Il n'est pas difficile de s'apercevoir si un homme est heureux ou malheureux.  La joie et la douleur sont ce qu'on dissimule le moins, surtout dans la jeunesse.*"[6]

HENRIETTE'S VOICE: Stop it!  Stop it, I said!  Grandmother!  Osamu's throwing persimmons at me!  *(Excitedly)*: All right for you!  Take that!

*A long silence.*

DOWAGER: *"Ils étaient jaloux, haineux, ambiteux.  J'étais indulgent et paisible; j'ignorais l'ambition.*"[7]

HENRIETTE'S VOICE: Osamu, be careful!  You're taking an awful risk!

DOWAGER: *"Il y a de ces passions violentes qui font les grand hommes et dont je n'avais pas l'étoffe.*"[8]

HENRIETTE'S VOICE: Grandmother, Osamu is eating the skins!  He'll make himself sick, won't he?  Osamu, you really are impossible!

*Dowager begins to show signs of awareness.  She raises her eyes from her book and occasionally looks in the direction of Henriette's voice.*

HENRIETTE'S VOICE: Grandmother!

DOWAGER: What is it?  Must you make such a racket?

---

lacked confidence.  That seriously handicapped me with women."

[3] "For I judged that a woman's cardinal sin was not to be good looking."

[4] "I observed that many young men who did not come up to me got on better and were more popular in society than I."

[5] "I have always held that the one sensible thing in life is to seek for pleasure. . . ."

[6] "It is not difficult to tell whether a man is happy or unhappy.  Joy and sorrow are things a man is least prone to conceal, especially when he is young."

[7] "They were jealous, spiteful, and ambitious.  I was indulgent and peace-loving; I did not know what ambition was."

[8] "There are passions that mould great men, passions of a stuff whereof I could

HENRIETTE: Grandmother! *(She enters.)* Grandmother, Osamu's climbed all the way to the top of the tree and says he's going to take a nap. He's got his eyes closed and his arms crossed and he's just lying there. I tried poking him, but he won't get up.

DOWAGER: That's no place to play. Go and tell him to come down this instant.

*Henriette exits, giggling.*

*Dowager goes on reading in silence.*

HENRIETTE'S VOICE: Osamu! Hurry up and pick the ones you want. It's getting dark. *(Pause.)* No, no, more to left. To the left. The left, I said. That's it. You've got your hand right on it, can't you tell? There, there . . . yes, that's the one!

DOWAGER *(once again reading out loud to herself)*: *"Mais ce dont je m'aperçus après une longue observation, c'est ques le désir embellit les objets sur lesquels il pose ses ailes de feu, que sa satisfaction, décevante le plus souvent, est la ruine de l'illusion, seul vrai bien des hommes."*[9]

HENRIETTE'S VOICE: That's enough. Really. That's plenty. *(She begins to sound alarmed)*: Come on, stop it now. If you go any higher, it really will be dangerous. Osamu, please! I said that's enough! *(She begins to whimper. Then suddenly, her voice rising)*: Grandmother! Osamu won't listen to me. He's climbing all the way up to the top of the tree, right up into the thin branches!

DOWAGER *(concerned)*: Osamu, that's quite enough!

*A long pause.*

HENRIETTE'S VOICE: See, I told you so! *(Pause.)* What? All together? A lot. Let me see: one, two, three, four, five, six, seven, eight, nine, ten, eleven, twelve, thirteen. . . .

DOWAGER *(reading again, somewhat louder than before)*:
*"O Thébains! Jusqu'au jour qui termine la vie*
*Ne regardons personne avec un oeil d'envie.*
*Peut-on jamais prévoir les derniers coups du sort?*

---

not boast. . . . "

[9]"But what I came to perceive, after prolonged observation, was that desire lends an added beauty to the things over which it hovers with its wings of fire. And I further perceived that the satisfaction of it, being usually disappointing, destroys the illusion, illusion wherein man's true happiness alone resides. . . "

*Ne proclamons heureux nul homme avant sa mort.* "[10]

HENRIETTE'S VOICE: Now what are you doing? Why are you climbing up so high? Osamu, stop it! Those branches are dangerous; they're too weak! Please, come down!

*As if struck with a sudden sense of peril.  Dowager drops her book and instinctively covers her mouth.  She is already on her feet when she hears Henriette's voice scream, "Osamu, watch out!"*

*Curtain.*

---

[10]"O Thebans, till life's last day
Never let us look on anyone with the eye of envy.
Can one ever foresee the last blows of fate?
Call no man happy till he is dead."

## ACT TWO

*A morning toward the end of March the following year.*
   *The two chairs are aligned precisely as before. Dowager sits in one;*
*Henriette reclines in the other. Both have been reading; their books are on*
*their laps. They are silent, lost in thought.*
   *Henriette has a poultice around her throat.*
DOWAGER: Your aunt will be here from Hongô soon. Just say hello, and
   then go off and review your lessons for tomorrow.
HENRIETTE: Yes, but Hiroshi will be here at ten.
DOWAGER: You're still not ready for tennis, Henriette.
HENRIETTE: Why not?
DOWAGER: What do you mean why not? Today's the first day you've
   been without a fever.
HENRIETTE: Then how about a walk?
DOWAGER: You stay home today like a good girl. Next Sunday you can
   play tennis or anything you like. As for Hiroshi, he can listen to
   phonograph records with you.
HENRIETTE: Hiroshi doesn't like phonograph records.
DOWAGER: What does he like, then?
HENRIETTE: He says he's happy just listening to the sound of my voice.
DOWAGER *(trying not to laugh)*: You mean you sing for him?
HENRIETTE: Sometimes I sing. He gets cross when I'm quiet.
DOWAGER: What do you mean "cross"?
HENRIETTE: You know, annoyed.
DOWAGER: He sounds just the type for you. But now you can do me a
   favor and be quiet. I can't read a thing with you chattering on as you
   do.
HENRIETTE: But Grandmother, you're the one who. . . .
DOWAGER: Enough, my dear, or I'll personally sew your mouth shut!
*Pursing her lips as if they had been sewn together, Henriette laughs.*
   *Dowager ignores her and turns the pages of her book.*
   *Silence.*
TSURU *(entering)*: A letter has come for you, Madame.
DOWAGER *(taking the letter and opening it)*: Tsuru, would you call
   Hongô and see if my daughter has left yet?
TSURU: Yes, Madame. *(Exits.)*

*Dowager reads the letter. The envelope is covered with foreign stamps, and the text is quite lengthy. It clearly means a great deal and could only be from a family member. The contents of the letter also seem significant. Finally, it must be the sort of missive that fills the reader's heart with a plethora of inexpressible emotions.*

*Henriette stares at Dowager's face and quivering fingers, trying to assess her grandmother's emotions as she reads the letter.*

HENRIETTE *(unable to contain herself any longer)*: Is the letter from my father?

*Dowager nods silently.*

HENRIETTE *(exuberant)*: What about me? Isn't there anything for me?

*Dowager goes through the letter page by page, then looks into the envelope.*

DOWAGER: Oh, I'm sorry! This part's for you. Here, take it over there and read it.

HENRIETTE: Why can't I read it here?

DOWAGER: Of course you can read it here. Only do be quiet. *(She continues to scrutinize her portion.)*

*Like Dowager, Henriette becomes engrossed in her letter.*

*Dowager rereads the pages she has.*

*Tsuru enters.*

TSURU: I called Hongô. They say she left about an hour ago.

DOWAGER: Then she should be here any minute. See that things are ready for lunch, will you?

TSURU: Yes, Madame. *(She exits.)*

DOWAGER *(putting her pages back in the envelope)*: What does your father say?

HENRIETTE: Just a minute. It's hard to understand. I can't make out this part.

DOWAGER: Well, read it out loud.

HENRIETTE: No!

DOWAGER: You mean it's so private you can't even share it with me?

HENRIETTE: Grandmother! All right, if you tell me what he says in your part. Does he say anything about me?

DOWAGER: Of course he does. In fact, it's all about you.

HENRIETTE: Really? You wrote him about me, didn't you! You're terrible!

DOWAGER: Go ahead, let's hear what he has to say.

HENRIETTE: Well, I'll just read you the good parts. "I have been away on a trip, so I just received your letter of November 20. Both your vocabulary and your handwriting have improved." Who does he think he is? I just hate him! Let me see, I'll skip this part.   "Judging from the photograph you sent, you have put on some weight, but you look very pretty anyway." He's making fun of me! I don't like this part either. The whole thing is like that. I really don't want to read any of it! DOWAGER: It would be better if you'd stop editorializing and read it straight through, don't you think? HENRIETTE: All right. But just this part. "I was sorry to hear about Osamu. It must have been a terrible shock for you, too, being at the scene as you were. You say he paid no attention even though you told him to stop, so you can hardly be held responsible. Nevertheless, when you are with another person, you have to be careful or this kind of accident can happen. The fact that you weren't hurt is, I suppose, some consolation, but in any case, girls shouldn't climb trees." What does he mean, "girls shouldn't climb trees"! DOWAGER *(tears in her eyes)*: Is that all he says about Osamu? HENRIETTE: Yes. Let's see, I'll skip over this part. . . . DOWAGER: What part are you skipping? HENRIETTE: "Next time write to me in French. And don't have your grandmother correct your grammar!" Oops, now I have read too much! *At this moment, Tsuru ushers in Kazue. She is dressed in a conservative kimono appropriate to one in mourning.* KAZUE: Hello. How have you been? DOWAGER: Fine, thank you. And you? KAZUE: Studying hard, Henriette? *Henriette nods.* KAZUE: How is your cold? I hope you're feeling better. DOWAGER: The child hates being cooped up in the house. Sometimes she's really impossible. But you got here quickly, I must say! KAZUE: Well, I've been looking forward to coming. *(She looks around her.)* It's been a whole month since I was here last. Everything looks so much more like spring now. DOWAGER: Shall we go for a stroll? KAZUE: No, I'm quite comfortable here. *(She pulls up a chair and sits.)* HENRIETTE: Well, if you'll excuse me. *(She begins to leave.)* KAZUE: Oh, won't you sit with us? DOWAGER: It really isn't good for her to be out too long. We can  call her back later. *Henriette exits.*

KAZUE: I thought I had recovered. But when I come here, I don't know .
. . it just seems. . . . *(She dabs her eyes with a handkerchief.)*
DOWAGER: I understand.
*A long silence.*
KAZUE: I see you've had the persimmon tree cut down.
DOWAGER: It turned out to be quite an undertaking. Especially having
the trunk hauled away. It took an entire day. When I saw it lying
there, I realized how large a tree it was. I had the roots removed too.
I've been thinking of setting up a trellis with the kind of climbing
roses Osamu liked.
*Kazue is silent.*
DOWAGER: I know how you feel. I've been feeling so old since last
fall, immensely old.
KAZUE: Please, Mother! Compared to me, you're so young and alive!
Perhaps it's because you have something to live for.
DOWAGER: To live for?
KAZUE: Since the accident, I haven't had the slightest interest in books.
DOWAGER: My love for books is little consolation. In fact, it's really
rather pathological.
KAZUE: Pathological? I wish I had the same affliction. I really must
find something to occupy my mind. As a matter of fact, I've taken up
fabric-dyeing again. My designs are no good, but at least it helps me
pass the time.
DOWAGER: Don't be modest. I'll have to find an opportunity to drop by
and see what you've done. You really should get out more, though.
Have you thought about tennis?
KAZUE: Tennis? Me? What a sight that would be!
DOWAGER: It doesn't matter how you look. The point is, there's noth-
ing like a little physical exercise to lift the spirits.
*Kazue does not respond.*
DOWAGER: Music might be helpful too. But you need self-discipline for
music.
KAZUE: Yes, I need something I can do mechanically, without thinking.
DOWAGER: And preferably with another person.
*A long silence.*
KAZUE: Another person to do things with . . . I'd be so grateful for
someone like that.
*Another pause.*
DOWAGER: I think of Osamu. Perhaps it was because he'd been ill, but
the only time he seemed truly happy was when he was physically
active.

KAZUE: As a child, he never took much interest in sports.

DOWAGER: Perhaps not. First you have to take part; then you begin to enjoy yourself.

KAZUE: I think being with Henriette had as much to do with it as anything.

DOWAGER: It wasn't only because of her.

*The women fall silent.*

KAZUE: I don't think he'd ever climbed a tree before. Why on that day he had to go clambering up, I'll never know.

DOWAGER: There's no sense in speculating now. *(Showing Kazue the letter)*: Your brother Akira indulges himself the same way.

KAZUE: Akira knows?

DOWAGER: He says he received word on February 20. Apparently he was in Algeria all winter.

KAZUE: He never seems to tire of traveling, does he?

DOWAGER: He's been wandering around the Mediterranean for ten years now. He's even missed seeing his daughter grow up.

KAZUE: And he's always alone.

*Dowager is silent.*

KAZUE: Doesn't he ever think of having Henriette join him?

DOWAGER: What would be the point of a young girl spending her life traipsing after an archaeologist? If he were doing his research in Paris the way he used to, it would be different, but. . . .

*A long silence.*

KAZUE: I was rearranging the bookshelves yesterday. I found Osamu's diary.

DOWAGER: I never knew he kept a diary.

KAZUE: He wasn't very good about it. But in every entry, he writes "H" did this and "H" did that. At first, I didn't know who "H" was.

DOWAGER: Henriette, of course.

KAZUE: Yes, and that's the first I realized. . . .

*Pause.*

DOWAGER: *Pauvre garçon!*

*A long silence.*

KAZUE: I didn't have the slightest inkling. *(She pauses.)* It seemed to be tearing him apart.

DOWAGER: I'm grateful he kept his feelings to himself. He must have realized it wasn't meant to be.

KAZUE: But they were cousins. . . .

DOWAGER: Even so, I'm grateful he never let her know how he felt.

KAZUE: I suppose.

DOWAGER: Henriette's such a strong-headed girl, I wonder if she'd have been good for him. I know there's no sense speculating at this late date, but even so. . . .

KAZUE: I wonder if it's because she's half-European.

DOWAGER: What does that have to do with it?

KAZUE: I mean her temperament.

DOWAGER: Temperament? Her temperament resembles her father's.

KAZUE: Do you think so? Now that you mention it, Osamu took after his father, as well.

DOWAGER: Osamu was the younger son in your family, but he was so grown-up, everyone mistook him for his older brother. He was meant to die young. It seems so obvious to me these days. *(She places a chocolate bonbon in her mouth.)* Help yourself. These bonbons are excellent.

KAZUE: No, thanks.

*A phonograph record of the "Elegie" from Massanet's* Thaïs *is heard.*[11]

---

[11]First performed at the Paris Opera on March 16, 1894, *Thaïs* by Jules Massenet (1842-1912) is based on Anatole France's 1890 novel by the same title. Here is a synopsis: "Egypt, in the fourth century A.D. Act I. Scene I. The banks of the Nile. A refuge of the Cenobites. Athanaël (baritone) laments the corruption of the inhabitants of Alexandria and blames the beautiful courtesan Thaïs (soprano). In his dream he sees her and, when he wakes, he decides to save her from sins. Scene II. The terrace of Nicias's house in Alexandria. Athanaël tells his friend Nicias (tenor) of his mission. Nicias laughs at the idea, but as he is expecting Thaïs that evening, he invites Athanaël to speak to her then. Thaïs tries to seduce Athanaël, who indignantly repulses her. Act II. Scene I. Thaïs's house. The courtesan is horrified at the idea of growing old. Athanaël persuades her to reflect upon her dissolute life and she almost allows herself to be converted. Yet in the end she refuses to give up her way of life. Scene II. In front of Thaïs's house. Athanaël is sleeping on the steps. His arguments have deeply affected Thaïs, and she now asks him what to do to gain salvation. He urges her to go to a convent where Albine (contralto) has gathered together young women who live in retreat. He offers to take Thaïs there on condition that she burns everything belonging to her past life. Thaïs agrees and leaves her house in flames as she walks away, dressed in a simple woolen tunic. Act III. Scene I. An oasis in the desert. Athanaël hands Thaïs over to the nuns at Albine's convent and takes his leave of her, sad at the thought of not seeing her again. Scene II. The banks of the Nile. The Cenobites' retreat.

KAZUE: Is someone else here?

DOWAGER: It must be Hiroshi. He plays tennis with Henriette. A nice, mature young man.

KAZUE: Oh yes, he was here before, the out-going one.

DOWAGER: I'm afraid they're a bit too friendly, but what can you do? *(She smiles briefly.)*

KAZUE *(with some effort, she smiles as well)*: Nothing, I suppose.

*A long silence.*

DOWAGER: Akira pretends to be indifferent, but in fact he's quite concerned about the daughter he left behind. As a matter of fact, he raises all kinds of questions in his letter. For my part, I can see what's coming, and I have concerns of my own about keeping Henriette here with me indefinitely.

*Kazue does not respond.*

DOWAGER: Yvonne never could get used to the climate in Japan, and finally it cost her and Akira their marriage. But what could be sadder than a young girl without a mother to look after her? And all Yvonne gained for her trouble was a few phrases in Japanese.

KAZUE: Indeed.

DOWAGER: But why are we reviewing this unpleasant history today?

KAZUE: You took one look at me and realized how depressed I feel, that's why. I feel fine on my way over here, but somehow, when I arrive. . . .

*Running footsteps can be heard inside the house, and suddenly the window curtains are thrown back. Henriette appears in the aperture.*

HENRIETTE: Forgive me for not coming outside, but, Grandmother, Hiroshi says he's moving to Osaka!

DOWAGER: He is?

HENRIETTE: Why does he have to move?

DOWAGER: I don't know. Ask him to come out here.

---

Athanaël cannot forget Thaïs. Palémon (bass), an old Cenobite, reprimands him, urging him to resist the temptation of evil. Athanaël prays and goes to sleep. He dreams that Thaïs is dying, surrounded by nuns. He gets up confused and determined to see her once again. Scene III. Athanaël arrives just in time to see her before she dies. She recognizes him and thanks him for saving her. In despair he talks to her of his love for her, but she no longer understands what he means by his sensual earthly love for, as she dies, her thoughts are of celestial forgiveness." *The Simon and Schuster*

*Henriette hurries away from the window.*
DOWAGER: Did you see Henriette's face?
*Kazue nods.*
*The phonograph stops. Hiroshi and Henriette appear together.*
DOWAGER: Henriette says that you're moving to Osaka?
HIROSHI *(bowing politely to Kazue and Dowager)*: Yes, my father told
    me this morning. It was like a bolt out of the blue!
DOWAGER: Will you be working in Osaka?
HIROSHI: That's part of it . . . I mean, well, yes.
DOWAGER: Well, congratulations. Will you be working for a company?
    A bank?
HIROSHI: I really don't know. I guess they make you do a lot of differ-
    ent things at first.
DOWAGER: On-the-job training, is that it?   As I recall, you have  friends
    in Osaka?
HIROSHI: Yes, one of my father's associates. He's involved in a lot of
    different enterprises. I'll be staying with him. I guess you could say
    I'll be in his safe keeping.
DOWAGER: And when are you leaving?
HIROSHI: That's the strange part: this coming Monday. That doesn't
    even give me time to have a decent suit of clothes made.
DOWAGER: Monday . . . *(counting on her fingers)*: that's just four days
    from now. Was this totally unexpected?
HIROSHI: My going, you mean? Well, they have been talking about my
    joining the family for some time, but it was only talk.
DOWAGER: Why, Hiroshi, then you're going to Osaka to be married!
HIROSHI: Well, yes, when you come right down to it.[12]
*Henriette can hardly contain her tears.*
DOWAGER *(noticing the change in Henriette's expression)*: Henriette, go
    ask Tsuru if lunch is ready. We'll be eating soon.
*Henriette practically leaps away, like a lamb loosed from its tether.*
KAZUE: Not to pry, but the young lady in Osaka? . . .
HIROSHI *(indicating her height with his hands)*: Just a strip of a girl,
    really.

---

*Book of the Opera* (New York: Simon and Schuster, 1977), pp. 1893-1894.
[12]Hiroshi is marrying into a family as an adopted son. This is not an
    unusual situation in Japan, where families with no male heirs frequently

KAZUE: You're quite young yourself, after all. You'll make a wonderful couple.

*Hiroshi smiles broadly.*

DOWAGER: But you haven't actually committed yourself yet, have you?

HIROSHI: I might as well have. We're well passed the point of no return. On the other hand, if I got fed up, I wouldn't think twice about leaving her.

KAZUE: Hiroshi!

DOWAGER: I suppose you've been seeing the young lady?

HIROSHI: I've met her two or three times, yes. I mean, she's only sixteen.

DOWAGER: I'm sure she'll make a delightful bride.

HIROSHI: Hold on, I'm not getting married tomorrow!

DOWAGER *(laughing)*: I should think not. After all, there are preparations to be made, and. . . .

*Kazue smiles.*

HIROSHI *(scratching his head)*: They say it's rough being adopted into your wife's family.

DOWAGER: Not necessarily. But I suppose you won't be able to come up to Tokyo very often, will you?

HIROSHI *(brightly)*: Oh, yes I will! After all, I have to keep tabs on Henriette!

DOWAGER *(glancing back at Kazue)*: How very thoughtful of you.

HIROSHI: She'll be in Japan, won't she?

DOWAGER: Of course she will. She wouldn't go off and leave her aging grandmother behind. Would she, Kazue?

*Kazue shakes her head, her eyes smiling assent.*

HIROSHI *(unconvinced)*: But what if her father summoned her?

DOWAGER: Yes, there's always that possibility. Eventually I suppose I will be left alone.

KAZUE: Oh, Mother, I'll be here. Isn't that right, Hiroshi?

HIROSHI: Absolutely.

DOWAGER: I first realized five or six years ago how lonely it will be when I'm alone.

KAZUE: You're so dedicated, Mother. I could never be like you.

HIROSHI: My mother's the lonely type, too. She began weeping this morning and hasn't stopped since.

---

adopt a daughter's husband in order to perpetuate the family name.

KAZUE: You're the last to leave the nest, after all.

DOWAGER: Children just don't have any idea what they put their parents through.

*Kazue is silent.*

DOWAGER: When they're ready to leave, they just go. And when they're ready to die, they just die.

*Kazue smiles with forlorn identification.*

HIROSHI: Please! You make us sound like little ogres.

DOWAGER *(smiling)*: Don't you dare forget the house where you'd come each Sunday to play tennis, you hear?

KAZUE *(smiling but with effort)*: The house where a boy fell to his death from a persimmon tree.

DOWAGER: Yes.

HIROSHI *(lowering his eyes)*: I won't forget.

DOWAGER: Henriette will be lonesome too, without anyone to play tennis with.

*Henriette's weeping becomes audible inside the house. Everyone turns toward the window.*

DOWAGER *(a strained expression on her face)*: Hiroshi, I think we had better say good-bye for today. Before you leave for Osaka, please drop by and we'll have tea. Henriette is not feeling well, so you'll have to excuse us.

HIROSHI: Of course. *(He bows and leaves.)*

*Silence.*

DOWAGER *(calling)*: Henriette. *(There is no response.)* Henriette!

*Dowager rises and exits upstage. After a few moments, she returns, her arm around Henriette's shoulders, comforting her.*

KAZUE: Is everything all right?

DOWAGER *(resuming her seat, she takes Henriette on her knee and comforts her)*: There, there. It's not as if the world's come to an end, is it?

*Henriette buries her face in her grandmother's breast. Then, without a word she leaps to her feet and rushes inside. The sound of footsteps ascending the stairs.*

*Disconcerted, Dowager looks at Kazue. A certain presentiment clouds her face momentarily, and she rises abruptly from her chair. But then, reconsidering, she follows Henriette with slow, deliberate steps.*

*Left by herself, Kazue rises instinctively from her chair and stands looking up at the second story of the house.*

*A long silence.*

*Eventually Dowager returns, walking with the same deliberate gait. She looks tired but also profoundly relieved.*

KAZUE: Is everything all right?

DOWAGER: Hm? You mean Henriette? *(Not answering this question)*: It would never have worked anyway.

KAZUE: But, Mother. That's the way of the world.

DOWAGER *(with a sigh)*: I was afraid it was happening all over again.

KAZUE: Happening again?

DOWAGER: Let her cry her heart out. Women, young women, are lucky: they can wash their losses away with their tears.

*Curtain.*

## ACT THREE

*An autumn afternoon the same year. The poplars have completely lost their leaves.*

*The windows of the house are open. One cannot see inside very clearly, but the Dowager can be observed bustling in and out.*

*"Grandmother, can you come here for a minute?" It is Henriette's voice calling from the second floor.*

*Tsuru is also busily going in and out of the house.*

*Finally, Henriette appears, dressed for an excursion. She is followed by Dowager and then by Tsuru.*

DOWAGER *(looking at her watch)*: We've still got plenty of time. If we left now, we'd have more than a hour to wait.

HENRIETTE: It's always better to be a bit early. Anyway, Aunt Kazue said she'd be there by five.

DOWAGER: Oh, before I forget. Your father might kiss you when he sees you, so don't be surprised.

HENRIETTE: Don't worry. I remember when Father left. His beard was so scratchy, it hurt my face! Aren't you going to kiss him, Grandmother?

DOWAGER: I'd like to, but I'm afraid if I did it would be your father who'd be surprised.

*As Dowager says this, she suddenly puts one hand to her forehead and the other hand on Henriette's shoulder. She staggers and pitches forward. Henriette and Tsuru catch and support her.*

HENRIETTE: Grandmother!

TSURU: Madame!

*The two manage to help her into a chair.*

TSURU: Shall I call the doctor?

HENRIETTE: Yes, use the telephone. Dr. Mizoguchi. And hurry!

*Tsuru hurries off.*

HENRIETTE *(tears in her voice)*: Grandmother, what's wrong? Is there some medicine? . . .

*Dowager waves her away weakly.*

HENRIETTE *(putting her hand on Dowager's forehead)*: Shouldn't you put your head down?

DOWAGER *(gently)*:  You just rushed me so.  *(Pause.)*  There's nothing to worry about.

*A long silence.*

HENRIETTE:  Shall I call Aunt Kazue and tell her we'll be late?

DOWAGER: Just let me rest a minute.  I'll be all right.

*Tsuru reappears.*

TSURU: The doctor will be here right away.  He was just on his way out, he said.

DOWAGER:  Doctor?  I just felt dizzy for a moment, that's all.  There's no need to involve the doctor.  I do feel rather thirsty though.  Tsuru, bring me a cup of hot tea, will you?

TSURU: Of course.  *(Exits.)*

HENRIETTE:  Perhaps you'd better not go today.

DOWAGER:  There's nothing wrong with me that a few moments rest won't cure.  How could I face your father if I didn't meet him at the station?

HENRIETTE: But we'll all be late if. . . .

DOWAGER:  Relax, Henriette, there's plenty of time.  You're not the only one who's anxious to see your father.  And he'll be disappointed, too, if you're the only one who's there to meet him.

*A long silence.*

*Tsuru brings the tea.*

DOWAGER *(quietly sipping the tea)*:  Straighten up the parlor.  And when you're done with that, don't forget to change the light bulbs in the dining room.

TSURU: Yes, Madame.

DOWAGER *(feeling her own pulse and then almost to herself)*:  When you get old, you lose all modesty.  Henriette, I'm sorry I was short with you just now.  I didn't mean to be.  Your father's coming home to see you and you alone.  When he steps off that train, I want you to be the first to greet him and welcome him back.  Then what do you think he'll say?  He'll wrap his arms around you and say, "Dear Henriette, you've been so good and patient while I've been gone."  Then he'll stroke your cheeks and say, "How like your mother you look.  Exactly like her."  *(Pause.)*  Tsuru, I'm feeling much better now.  You go ahead and get dinner ready.  Isn't Yoshi back yet?

TSURU: No, it takes her forever to run a simple errand.

DOWAGER: Look who's talking!  Now, this is no place to receive the doctor.  I'll wait for him upstairs.  *(She looks at her watch.)*  We still have twenty minutes before we have to leave.  Plenty of time.  *(She tries to get up but falls back into her chair.*) How very peculiar. I guess I'm still not myself.

HENRIETTE: You had better stay where you are for a little while longer.

*ing away for a sign of the Doctor*): Are you feeling faint?

DOWAGER: No, as long as I'm sitting like this, I'm fine. I wonder if there isn't someone who could carry me to Tokyo Station?

HENRIETTE *(amused)*: Chair and all?

DOWAGER: Yes, chair and all. Wouldn't people be amazed?

HENRIETTE: They'd crowd around you.

DOWAGER: When they realized it was a pitiful old woman who'd come to welcome her son home, though, they wouldn't dare laugh. Henriette, hand me that stole, would you?

*Henriette drapes the fur stole about Dowager's shoulders.*

DOWAGER: My legs are still cold. Isn't there something else I could put on?

*Tsuru goes inside.*

HENRIETTE: Grandmother, stop fidgeting.

DOWAGER: Why don't you sit down yourself? You'll wear yourself out standing up like that. *(She pampers Henriette, tucking loose strands of hair under her bonnet.)* This hat suits you so well. Look over that way. Beautiful. Now, when you meet your father, what are you going to say?

*Henriette squirms, unable to find the words.*

DOWAGER: Come now, what will you say to him? You don't plan to just stand there squirming!

HENRIETTE: Will there be a lot of other people?

DOWAGER: It's hard to say. Knowing your father, he may not have let anyone know he's coming. Of course, there was that article in the newspaper, but even so, people would have no way of knowing his exact time of arrival. I wonder what his relations are with his old friends these days.

HENRIETTE: But Father is a famous scholar, isn't he?

DOWAGER: In France, yes. But that's precisely why he's not accepted here. Look at Osamu's father. He was hardly thirty when he received his doctorate, but your father was merciless with him. Why scholars in different disciplines have to go to such lengths to belittle each other, I'll never understand.

HENRIETTE: Osamu's father was an anthropologist, wasn't he?

DOWAGER: That's right. But today, your father's one of the world's leading archaeologists.

*Tsuru enters with a down quilt.*

TSURU *(wrapping the Dowager in it)*: Madame, the doctor is here.
DOWAGER: Ask him if he'd be so kind as to see me here.
*Tsuru exits. She returns shortly with the Doctor.*
DOCTOR: Now, what seems to be the trouble?
DOWAGER *(with a show of fine spirits)*: Nothing, really. A spell of dizziness is all. I suppose all the excitement recently has taken its toll.
DOCTOR: Yes, I understand your son is arriving today. Were you on your way to the station?
DOWAGER: Yes, we were just about to leave when I suddenly felt faint, and I've been resting here ever since.
DOCTOR: You can't be very comfortable in that chair. Do you still feel dizzy?
DOWAGER: As a matter of fact, I would have preferred to receive you inside, but when I tried to stand just now, for some reason. . . .
DOCTOR *(taking her pulse)*: I see. . . .
DOWAGER: I knew it was coming, but honestly. . . .
DOCTOR: Now, now, don't jump to conclusions. There's really nothing very much the matter with you.
DOWAGER: Then I'm not going to. . . .
DOCTOR: No, no, just a little cerebral anemia would be my guess. You've been under a strain recently, after all.
DOWAGER: Yes, what with Osamu's death. . . .
DOCTOR: Let me have a look at your tongue. Ah, fine, just fine. *(After examining her eyes)*: Now, let's check your heart, just in case. *(He places his stethoscope on her chest.)* Regular as clockwork. You have nothing to worry about. But for safety's sake, I'd suggest you stay quiet for the remainder of the day.
DOWAGER: Then I won't be able to go to the station?
DOCTOR: Caution really would be the best policy. From what I've seen, I can only recommend that you remain at home.
DOWAGER: And if I decide to, let us say, exert myself a little?
DOCTOR: Absolutely not. After all, you've been living here in retirement for some time. And now, to have all this activity thrust upon you. I realize what a special occasion this is, but I must insist that you bear with the situation as best you can. *(Shaking his head at her)*: But this is a surprise! Who would have thought I'd need to speak to you of all people like this! You can't rely on anyone anymore.
DOWAGER: I'm afraid I just can't help myself. My son's returning, and. . . .
DOCTOR: Of course, I understand.

DOWAGER *(wiping away her tears)*: Very well, so be it. Henriette, you go on alone. You can manage to find your way, can't you? Find your Aunt Kazue and have her help you look for your father. Would you like Tsuru to go with you?

HENRIETTE: No, I'll be fine.

DOWAGER: You won't get lost on the way, will you? I'd feel much better if Tsuru were with you.

HENRIETTE: Don't worry, Grandmother, I can find my way to Tokyo Station!

DOWAGER: All right then. Your aunt will be waiting in the lady's waiting room. You still have plenty of time, so you needn't rush.

HENRIETTE: I wonder what Father will be wearing?

DOWAGER: That's hard to say. You don't remember what he looks like, do you? It's been a long time, but your aunt shouldn't have any trouble recognizing him. *(Thinking)*: I know, take this photo-graph with you and compare it to the passengers as they leave the train. *ing, she removes the locket she wears and places it around Henriette's neck.)*

*Henriette examines the photograph minutely.*

DOWAGER: He has a mole on the side of his nose. Look for that. *(Smiling at the Doctor)*: This is getting to sound like one of those old-fashioned stories about children setting out to find their long-lost parents. *(To Henriette)*: When your aunt asks you what happened, just tell her I wasn't feeling well. Under no circumstances are you to tell your father that I had a dizzy spell and collapsed as I was leaving home. Now, you'd better be on your way before it get's too late. *(To Tsuru)*: Now where did that chauffeur go?

*Tsuru hurries off.*

HENRIETTE *(cheerfully)*: Well, I'm off! *(She exits in high spirits.)*

*Dowager watches her go in silence.*

*A long pause.*

DOCTOR: What a pleasure to see such a fine daughter after all these years!

DOWAGER: My son? He'll be beside himself. He won't give a thought to his old mother, lying here waiting, waiting. . . .

DOCTOR: Come now, you know he cares for you. It's just not the same thing.

*A long silence.*

DOWAGER: It's been just a year since the last time we had to call you here in an emergency.

DOCTOR: Yes. And in both cases, my presence was unnecessary, albeit for different reasons. Last year there wasn't anything anyone could do.

DOWAGER: I was sitting here, right here, reading a book at the time.

DOCTOR: It must have been a terrible shock.

DOWAGER: It was so strange. I knew my grandson--Osamu was his name--I knew he was climbing the tree to pick persimmons. I knew how dangerous it was, and I knew that he should stop at once. But even though I knew it, I did nothing to stop him. I just went on, lost in my reading.

DOCTOR: That sort of thing happens. As I recall, your granddaughter was there as well.

DOWAGER: Yes, she was shouting to me about what Osamu was doing, and I could hear her quite distinctly, but for some reason the words just didn't register. I seem to recall warning Osamu once or twice myself, but somehow. . . .

DOCTOR: That's the way it is with accidents. They happen precisely because they couldn't be prevented.

DOWAGER: That's just the point. As I look back on it, I don't think it was a simple accident. I don't know whether I should tell you this, but. . . .

DOCTOR: No, perhaps you had better not. A doctor's task is to take the necessary steps in the circumstances at hand. Any extraneous knowledge would only complicate matters. Besides, if you talk any more, you'll only tire yourself. You rest here a few more minutes, and then I'll see you to your room. It's getting chilly out here.

DOWAGER: I had the persimmon tree cut down and hauled away.

DOCTOR: So I understand.

DOWAGER: I had a climbing rose planted in its place, but it wouldn't take. Osamu was so fond of those flowers.

DOCTOR: I see. *(He takes her pulse.)*

*A long silence.*

DOWAGER: Doctor, my heart is throbbing so, I can hardly. . . .

*Doctor does not respond but again checks her pulse.*

    *Tsuru enters.*

TSURU *(to Doctor)*: Is there anything I can do?

DOCTOR: Yes, as a matter of fact. Drop by my house, and have my assistant prepare this for me. *(He writes something on a scrap of paper and hands it to Tsuru.)*

TSURU: Right away. *(She exits.)*

DOCTOR: How do you feel now?

DOWAGER: My head aches.

DOCTOR: Just relax. You'll feel better in no time. When is the train due to arrive?

DOWAGER: At half-past five.

DOCTOR *(looking at his watch)*: Half-past five.

DOWAGER: Do I have enough time?

DOCTOR: Pardon me?

DOWAGER: Don't try to conceal it. Be honest with me.

DOCTOR: Be honest with you?

DOWAGER: Just the bare essentials. *(She draws in a deep breath.)*

DOCTOR: I'm afraid I really don't understand.

DOWAGER: How much longer do I have to? . . .

DOCTOR: Dear lady, that's hardly funny!

DOWAGER *(with difficulty)*: I don't want to die here.

DOCTOR: I'll move you presently.

DOWAGER *(calling)*: Tsuru!

DOCTOR: The maid has. . . .

*Tsuru enters hurriedly.*

DOWAGER: Tsuru, take me to my room.

DOCTOR *(to Tsuru)*: Just a minute. *(To Dowager)*: My dear lady, your condition really isn't that serious. This sort of thing happens all the time.

DOWAGER: To everyone, I should think.

DOCTOR: Before we take you upstairs, though, I would like to give you a little camphor.

DOWAGER: You mean an injection?

DOCTOR: Yes, just as a precaution.

DOWAGER: Please spare me. I can do without the additional pain.

DOCTOR: You really should cooperate.

DOWAGER: All right, then, I'll rest here as you suggest.

DOCTOR: If you'll promise that much, I'll have no complaints. *(To Tsuru)*: Is her bed ready?

TSURU: Yes, sir.

DOCTOR: Her room's on the second floor, isn't it? *(Pause.)* Let me see. . . . *(He considers)*: Would it be possible to bring some bedding down here? She really should rest like this a while longer.

*Tsuru goes inside. She returns shortly with two or three cushions.*

DOCTOR: Thank you, these are perfect. *(He puts one under her hips, another under her head, and so forth.)* Do you feel any discomfort?

DOWAGER: My head. . . .

DOCTOR *(taking her pulse)*: There is nothing to worry about. Perhaps you're concerned because I've been advising you about your heart, but as you can see, your pulse is strong as ever. There is absolutely nothing to be afraid of. You don't even show much in the way of a hardening of the arteries. *(Pause.)* See, the color is coming back into your face. *(To Tsuru)*: Do you have any whiskey in the house? Wine would do as well.

TSURU: We have some wine.

DOCTOR: Please.

*Tsuru goes inside. When she comes out, she is carrying a bottle of wine. Doctor pours some for Dowager to drink.*

DOCTOR: I see that you're not completely unaccustomed to alcohol. *(He examines the bottle.)* "Howt-sow-turn"?

TSURU: I think it's pronounced "*Haute sauterne*," Doctor.

DOCTOR *(looking at Tsuru)*: My word, you've become a real cosmopolitan working here!

*Tsuru covers her mouth to conceal an embarrassed smile. She quickly recovers, however, and becomes serious again.*

TSURU: Aren't you cold, Madame?

DOCTOR: Yes, perhaps another blanket would be a good idea. *(He puts a thermometer under her arm.)*

*Tsuru goes inside and brings out another quilt.*

DOWAGER: Doctor, aren't you cold?

DOCTOR: No, I'm afraid I'm too stout for that.

DOWAGER: The train must have arrived by this time.

DOCTOR: It's exactly five o'clock.

*Dowager is silent.*

DOCTOR: It's a shame you had to have this episode today of all days.

DOWAGER: I'll tell you what's a shame. I've lost a son, a daughter-in-law, and a grandson. And my other son abandoned me ten years ago and has been roaming the world ever since without the slightest sense of compunction. But I have had one consolation--the granddaughter you met before. I have loved her and cherished her like the unique treasure that she is. But today, this total stranger is going to come and deprive me of her as well. And he is a total stranger. I'm not speaking of my son who's returning from abroad, but another man, another man who is appearing out of nowhere claiming to be my son, a man with the unmitigated gall to claim he's a son of mine.

*The Doctor is silent.*

DOWAGER: He's going to claim Henriette as his daughter and steal her away from me.  No son of mine would do such a thing!  Would he, Doctor?

*Doctor removes the thermometer and reads it.  He cocks his head and looks uneasy.*

DOWAGER: I have as much as committed murder for Henriette.  I mean my grandson.  I loved him.  He was a boy who'd lost his father, a lonely boy who lived his whole life under a cloud because of his loss.  But I did it.  I killed Osamu.  *(She gasps for breath.)*

DOCTOR: Dear Lady!

DOWAGER: I did it--I pushed him from that persimmon tree.  Henriette's heart was dangling there, red, ready to be plucked!

DOCTOR: Please! . . .

DOWAGER *(almost inaudibly)*: My head!  My head!

*A long silence.*

DOWAGER *(increasingly agitated)*: Kazue, forgive me!  Your precious only son was in love with Henriette, but by then she had discovered Hiroshi.  And Hiroshi was in love with her too.  I was convinced of it, and then last spring, Kazue, you alone know the tragedy I had to witness!

*Doctor takes her pulse.*

DOWAGER: You were thinking about Osamu, and you looked at me with those eyes.  You don't know how I've tried to avoid those eyes of yours.  You'll probably protest that you don't know what I'm talking about.  Who could know?  But you were his mother, and with your mother's sixth sense you detected my guilt!

*Doctor is becoming more and more alarmed.*

*Dowager is having difficulty breathing, but she manages to speak in a clear voice.*

DOWAGER: *"O Thébains! Jusqu'au jour qui termine la vie."*

*A long silence.*

*Tsuru returns with a small box of medical supplies wrapped in white cloth.  She hesitantly approaches Doctor, hands him the package, and whispers a message.  Doctor nods.*

DOCTOR *(speaking into Dowager's ear)*: I think we can move you now.

DOWAGER: Do be quiet!  Henriette!  You and your father go anywhere you like!  I can see you have no more use for me!  Fine, I'll go somewhere where I'll be out of your way!

DOCTOR: It wouldn't do for you to catch cold. . . .

DOWAGER: Henriette, why are you always looking away from me?  Have I made you angry?  There's nothing to be so angry about.

*Signalling to Tsuru, Doctor begins raising Dowager to a sitting position.*
*Tsuru assists him from the opposite side.*

DOCTOR *(alarmed)*:  Oh, no!  *(He releases Dowager and immediately*
*begins to prepare an injection.)*  The family lives in Hongô, isn't that
right?  Do they have a telephone?

TSURU: Yes.

DOCTOR:  Try not to alarm them, but tell them to get here as quickly as
possible.

TSURU: May I tell them she's ill?

DOCTOR: Of course.

TSURU: I'm afraid the lady of the house has already left for the station to
meet Madame's son.

DOCTOR: And are they planning to come back here afterwards?

TSURU: I really couldn't say.

DOCTOR: In any case, call and leave word.  Is there anyone else who
should be notified?

TSURU: I'm afraid. . . .

DOCTOR:  All right.  Just go ahead and call Hongô then.

*Tsuru hurries off.  Doctor administers the injection.*

DOWAGER: Henriette . . . Henriette!

DOCTOR: She'll be back soon.  It won't be long.

DOWAGER: Osamu, why are you making that face?  There's nobody over
that way.

*Doctor takes her pulse again.*

*A long silence.*

*Rays from the setting sun bathe the scene and cast a somber glow over*
*Dowager's face.*

DOWAGER *(regaining some of her composure)*: There you are, my son!
A moment later, and I'd have missed you.  Come, come closer.  How
was your journey?  The seas weren't too rough, I hope.  *(Pause.)*
How wonderful to have you home at last.  It took you so long, I was
afraid you'd lost your way.  But look at you, you're covered with
dust!  *(Another long pause.)*  Is everyone here then?  What about
Osamu?  Where's Osamu?  *(Pause.)*  Someone, find him, quickly! . .
. *(Pause.)*  Forgive me!  Please, all of you forgive me!  I just lived a
little too long, that's all.  That was all.

*The sun has set.  The stage darkens gradually.*

*Curtain.*

*Cloudburst* as performed by the Tokyo Engeki Ensemble, October 1988.

*Cloudburst* as performed by the Tokyo Engeki Ensemble, October 1988.

*The Two Daughters of Mr. Sawa,* Act Three, as performed by the Tokyo Engeki Ensemble, December 1988.

*Photographs compliments of the Tokyo Engeki Ensemble.*

# THE TWO DAUGHTERS OF MR. SAWA

(1935)

translated by

David G. Goodman

*Characters:*
Sawa Kazuhisa
Etsuko, his elder daughter
Aiko, his younger daughter
Okui Raku, a maid
Momoe, her child
Kamiya Noritake, an importer
Tadokoro Rikichi, a sailor and friend of Etsuko and Aiko's deceased
brother Hatsuo

*Time:*
The late 1920s.

*Place:*
Tokyo.

## ACT ONE

*The home of Sawa Kazuhisa (55), former vice-consul and current administrator of a certain Catholic sanatorium. It is a cheap, Western-style house of clapboard construction in the suburbs. The stage is the smallish living room-dining room of the house, with a balcony in front painted in white.*

*The furniture, though old and worn, appears comfortable. There are landscape paintings and plates displayed on the wall, and among them-- out of place as it may seem--is the framed photograph of a woman. It is the sad, unexceptional face of someone thirty-five or thirty-six, her hair piled on top of her head in a matronly style. On a shelf, a variety of Western knickknacks have been assembled, among them a white marble clock, obviously a prized souvenir; while from the balcony railing, the fading formal wear of the former vice-consul has been hung out to air.*

*It is an October afternoon.*

*Okui Raku (38), the maid, is investigating the bank book on the table.*

RAKU *(without taking her eyes from the book)*: Momoe! Momoe! Momoe!! *(As there is no answer, she gets up and goes toward the door. Just then, a young girl dressed in a sailor suit enters.)* I've been calling you. Where've you been? In the toilet?

*Momoe shakes her head but seems ill-at-ease.*

RAKU *(severely)*: You were upstairs, weren't you? Why do you do such things without permission? Remember, this is not your house.

*Momoe is silent.*

RAKU *(mollifying her anger)*: As soon as I'm done with this, I'll make us some tea. You go in the next room and read a magazine or some-thing until I'm through.

MOMOE: I'm bored all by myself. I won't look anymore, Mother, so let me come with you.

RAKU: Absolutely not. You'll just distract me.

MOMOE: But I came to help. *(Pause.)* Mother, how much are you get-ting paid a month? Shall I guess?

RAKU: I'd much prefer if you didn't.

MOMOE: I'm going to earn thirty yen a month the minute I get out of school, you'll see.

RAKU: I can hardly wait.

MOMOE: Uncle said it was a terrible waste keeping a girl like me in school.

RAKU: I couldn't agree more.

MOMOE: He said that I could be really popular in an all-women's revue.

RAKU: Momoe, your uncle's a fool. Well, I guess I'll leave this for later. Do me a favor and see how the fire in the brazier is doing. *(She shakes the dust from the clothes being aired and takes them into the recesses of the house.)*

*Momoe also disappears into the interior, but she reappears and pages through the bank book on the table. By turns she stares, purses her lips, and strains to keep from laughing. Eventually, there is the sound of footsteps in the hall. Momoe's face instantly assumes an air of innocence as she walks toward the balcony.*

*Raku enters, carrying a Cossack hat.*

MOMOE: What's that?

RAKU: I found it at the bottom of the trunk.

MOMOE: It must have been a hat.

RAKU: It's a shame. Look how the moths have eaten it!

MOMOE *(as if to herself)*: This place gives me the willies! Mr. Sawa wears hats like that, and there are pictures of his dead wife all over the place. Mother, the woman's been dead for ten years!

RAKU *(setting the hat out on the railing of the balcony)*: What's so odd about that? You're the strange one, a child of your age, sticking her nose into everything when she should be studying. *(Pause.)* It's getting late. Let's make that tea the next time. To make it up to you, it's not much, but here's some spending money. *(She takes a coin purse from the sash of her kimono and gives her daughter a single fifty-sen silver coin.)*

MOMOE: May I?

RAKU: Aren't we shy all of a sudden! If you're going to the cinema by yourself, I'll take it back right now.

MOMOE: Thanks, Mother. Good-bye!

RAKU: Give my regards to your aunt and uncle.

MOMOE: I know that much!

*Raku stops her daughter on her way out and straightens her clothes. Just then, Sawa Kazuhisa appears at the door.*

SAWA: Well, well, look who's here!

RAKU: Oh! You startled me! When did you get home? Was the door unlocked? *(She makes as if to chase her daughter out.)*

SAWA: We'll be having a guest in a few minutes, so get out that bottle of wine, will you? And then, I don't know whether he'll be staying for dinner, but get things ready so we can serve something simple, just in case. Sukiyaki would be nice. Fellow called me today and said he'd be visiting the hospital, so I told him to drop by the house if he was coming this way. I drop in on him all the time, but he's never been here. Where did Momoe go? Did you send her home already? I'd have given her a little something. Bring me my robe from upstairs, will you? I'm exhausted! *Très fatigué! (He lights a cigarette.)*

*After a short interval, Raku enters carrying a gaudy dressing gown. Sawa puts it on over his shirt, places his right hand on Raku's shoulder, and kisses her lightly on the cheek. She accepts the kiss without expression and draws away.*

RAKU *(loudly, to compensate for the fact that Sawa is hard of hearing)*: Would you like me to make the bitter tea?

SAWA: Yes, and make it strong. Oh, and the evening edition's in my coat pocket.

RAKU: I'll get it right away.

*Sawa slowly exhales the smoke of his cigarette as he watches Raku leave, then he begins to softly hum a folk melody. He takes the evening newspaper that Raku brings him and begins to read it. The tea arrives. He sips it noisily. The sun begins to set. There is the sound of an automobile stopping in front of the house.*

SAWA: That must be him. *(The doorbell rings.)* All right, all right! I'll get it. No, you go. And be polite.

*Raku goes to the door. While she is gone, Sawa once again takes up the the evening paper. He does so in order to settle his nerves. Then Raku returns with a calling card.*

SAWA *(as if surprised)*: Well, well, what do you know? By all means, show him in! *(Going to the door to meet his guest)*: Welcome! How good of you to come! Did you have any trouble finding the place?

*The guest is Kamiya Noritake (52), also a former official with the Foreign Ministry who is reputed to have made a considerable fortune in the import trade.*

KAMIYA: Not particularly, but I'm afraid I've come at a rather awkward time. You see, I have another engagement this evening, but there's something I really had to speak to you about first.

SAWA: Come now, make yourself at home. We really don't have much to offer, but how about joining me for some sukiyaki? It's been quite a while--we can relive our days in Paris. I even have an unopened bottle of *vin blanc*.

KAMIYA:   Whoa, not so fast! I'm afraid I really can't join you tonight. As I said, I have a previous engagement.

SAWA: What?

KAMIYA:   I said I have a previous engagement. To see someone.

SAWA: So what? So you've got a previous engagement. Cancel it. "Time means nothing to the Japanese." Your wife said just that once in her excellent Japanese.

KAMIYA *(looking around the room)*:   You've kept all sorts of souvenirs, haven't you? I remember everything here. That plate, for instance. We bought that together in Stockholm, didn't we? The only one left from the group that went to that conference is Kasahara. He just came back from Turkey the other day. Finally made it to the rank of chief consul. But how are things with you, here at the hospital? Have you gotten used to your new life? Which is easier, this or stamping passports?

SAWA:   It's an interesting experience, living with the smell of formaldehyde twenty-four hours a day. When I go out, I feel like I've lost my sense of smell. I don't have anything to boast about, but at least I'm chief administrator and my age commands a certain amount of respect. Nobody here knows that I was dismissed from the foreign service the minute I made vice-consul. And I can capitalize on the fact that I spent twenty years abroad--that impresses people. I don't have any trouble bamboozling the young doctors. *(To Raku, who has just come in with tea)* Take that away and bring us some wine. We're going to live like the plebes tonight. Have you forgotten how we used to yell in that café in Crêpère before we got paid? *"Hé, garçon! Deux blancs!"*

KAMIYA:   After we'd lost at the race track, too. As a matter of fact, there she is. *(Looking at the woman's photograph on the wall)*: Your wife's the one who really had to pay for our carousing. You used to get advances against her home allowance and leave her with next to nothing.

SAWA *(removing the cork from the bottle of wine)*:   That was nothing. She didn't know real hardship until I was sacked in Madrid. There was a period of ten years when I was completely derelict in my responsibilities. But my wife never complained. I crossed over to Algeria and was going to make a fresh start when the Great War started. Come on, have a drink! Anyway, my scheme failed, and I didn't even have enough money to return home. I was desperate, so.

. . .

KAMIYA:  You joined the Foreign Legion, right? I've heard that story.

SAWA: Here's to old times! *(He raises his glass.)*

KAMIYA *(responding in kind)*:  To the *Légion d'honneur*!

SAWA:  It was the summer of 1924.  I got word that my wife was dying, so. . . .

KAMIYA:  Actually, that's what I wanted to discuss with you.

SAWA:  What?

KAMIYA:  Are your daughters still at work?  What time will they be home?

SAWA:  The older one's supposed to teach night school tonight.  The younger one should be home any minute.

KAMIYA:  Do they even make her teach nights?

SAWA:  Seems she volunteered.  I understand she's even working without pay.

KAMIYA:  Since you lost your son, I guess you'll be looking for someone to carry on the family name when you consider husbands for Etsuko?

SAWA: *Oh, non, merci!*

KAMIYA:  Good, then  you're on my  side.  Actually, that's what I wanted to talk to you about.  How would you feel about marrying Aiko off first?

SAWA:  By the way, thanks for all you did for Aiko.  She's very  grateful, believe me.  Girls these days seem to be proud to be out   working. And a record company to boot--she's lucky to have such  a glamorous job.  How's she doing?  Is she working out all right?

KAMIYA:  Of course.  Kisaki, the president of the company, is really going out of his way for her.  And I hear she's very efficient, too. I'm sure she'll do just fine, but when you consider the future, all kinds of new worries crop up.  A woman still needs a husband, after all.  Since I've already involved myself in her  affairs, I wondered how you'd react to my putting this efficient daughter of yours on the bejewelled palanquin to matrimonial bliss?

SAWA:  Bejewelled palanquin?

KAMIYA:  The fellow I have  in mind is a foreigner, it's true, but he's a viscount.  I'll show you  his card, and  you'll notice the five-starred crown printed in the upper left-hand  corner.  On top of that, I might mention that he's assistant manager of the Maison Perchée, and you'll understand that he's not in a bad financial position, either.

SAWA:  The assistant manager of what?

KAMIYA:  Perchée.  Don't  you  know  it?  They  have  a  branch  in Yokohama.

SAWA: French?

KAMIYA: Don't be a boor, *Légion d'honneur!*

SAWA: Don't keep bringing that up. Where did he meet her?

KAMIYA: If you're thinking it was at a dance hall, think again. Actually, this fellow likes to sing Japanese popular songs. As a matter of fact, he's really quite good at it, so I recommended him to National Records. It's not that a foreigner's never recorded Japanese songs before, but the feel of the songs is completely unique, and the president of the company got all excited about the idea. So I took this fellow over to their studios and had him make a recording. Anyway, your daughter was in charge of hospitality, if you know what I mean, and she was really very *charmante.* "Everything's ready, gentlemen. If you'll follow me." She charmed the hell out of him. Ever since, it seems he spends half his time at the record company. Before I forget, the young man's thirty-seven--thirty-eight by Japanese reckoning. His name's René de Beauchois, and like his name he's a real *bourgeois gentilhomme.* As I started to say before, I'm told he owns an enormous tract of land in Morocco along with a tannery.

SAWA: A what?

KAMIYA: A tannery, you know, for making leather.

SAWA: Sounds more like a cowhide palanquin to matrimonial bliss.

*Kamiya is does not react to this.*

SAWA: I see. No, I'm not particularly averse to the idea. But even at this, I'm still a Japanese, and the idea of pushing my daughter into the arms of some foreigner . . . it seems somehow disreputable, if you know what I mean. It'd be different if they'd come to the decision themselves. Try to understand. You know, it's funny, but the more I try to respect my daughters' wishes, the more my need to maintain some semblance of patriarchal dignity makes a coward of me. My rule is absolute noninterference, but as a result, even when I want to do something for them, I find myself tiptoeing around as if I were treading on thin ice. As you know, they have no mother, and. . . .

KAMIYA: Come come, you sound desperate!

SAWA: I don't mean to. I just don't have the courage to assert myself, that's all. I'm even reticent about living with the girls. As a matter of fact, not long ago I told them to get a taste of freedom and asked them if they didn't want to try apartment living. But they just looked at each other and wouldn't hear of it. I asked them why, and they said it was because they didn't want to use the money they earned for rent. Of course, it would be out of the question for a man in my position to try to cover their expenses completely. So I asked them how it would be if I gave them the seventy-odd yen I get each month for my pension. And this time do you know what they said?

KAMIYA: They had no objections, of course.

SAWA: No objections! But if I was going to give them the money anyway, they said, they'd rather go on living with me and keep the full amount for spending money.

KAMIYA: Why do they need so much money?

SAWA: The older one seems to have developed a rather peculiar hobby.

KAMIYA: Hobby?

SAWA: Charity. She gives it away.

KAMIYA: Really? That is unusual.

SAWA: Anyway, the point is that one thing led to another, and somehow it was decided that I would give them the seventy-odd yen as an allowance. But do you think I parcel it out grudgingly? *Au contraire!* I'm so easily intimidated--I guess I'm afraid that someday they won't take it--I just hand it over without even looking them in the eye.

KAMIYA: I suppose the doctors don't take much of an interest in your circumstances, do they?

SAWA: Actually, these days I'm a little strapped for funds, and I have to be careful not to give myself away. I'm afraid the girls are already laughing at me behind my back for being too proud to admit I'm broke.

KAMIYA: They're laughing, all right. You're such a spectacle, I can't help laughing myself.

SAWA: In that case, drink up! *(He tries to pour some more wine.)*

KAMIYA: No, thanks, I've had enough. Listening to you, you'd think there was no greater calamity in life than having children.

SAWA: And it follows that you are the happiest man in the world. Does your wife still beat you?

KAMIYA: That old battle-ax? She could be dead for all I care.

SAWA: Would you really rather be single?

KAMIYA *(glancing behind him at the entrance)*: It sounds like someone's here. I guess I'd better be going.

SAWA: Don't be silly, it's just the girls. This is a perfect chance for you to tease them a little. Only keep our little discussion under your hat.

*Raku appears.*

RAKU: The young ladies have just returned. *(In a louder voice)*: I say, your daughters. . . .

SAWA: I heard you. Tell them that Mr. Kamiya's here.

*The two sisters, Etsuko and Aiko, enter. The elder sister wears a kimono; the younger one wears Western-style clothes. The older girl, who at first glance seems to be dressed more conservatively, has a sunny air about her, while her sister seems aloof despite her gay attire.*

SAWA: What happened? You're home early today.

ETSUKO: A little bird told us we had a visitor. Right, Aiko?

AIKO *(to Kamiya)*: How very nice to see you.

KAMIYA: Hello! I can't remember when I last saw the two of you together like this.

SAWA: At Hatsuo's funeral. You came to the temple. That must have been the last time.

KAMIYA: Last spring, of course. I want you to know I hear nothing but good things about both of you.

AIKO: Is that so? Where?

KAMIYA: Everywhere! By the way, has young Monsieur Beauchois dropped by the office lately?

AIKO: You mean the European gentleman? Yes, he drops in from time to time.

KAMIYA: He's a fine young man, don't you think, relatively well-mannered. . . . He's a French nobleman, you know.

AIKO: Yes, he makes a point of that himself.

KAMIYA: Does he really? These French are incorrigible!

SAWA *(proudly)*: There's nothing quite like the French! *(To Etsuko)* I thought you had to teach tonight.

ETSUKO: I found somebody to substitute for me. Aiko says she wants to go to a movie tonight and won't listen to anything I say.

KAMIYA: Next time, allow me the pleasure of going with you.

ETSUKO: Oh, but you will be staying with us for a while today, won't you?

SAWA: This school where Etsuko teaches, it seems that there are quite a number of children from the poorer classes in attendance. I've been trying to persuade her to have them transfer her to a better school, but. . . .

ETSUKO: If the school were any better, *I* wouldn't make the grade.

KAMIYA *(to Etsuko)*: I may just be imagining things, but you seem a little tired. Working with children seems exciting on the surface, but actually it's one of the least glamorous jobs there is. After I graduated from middle school, I spent two years working in a country school myself you know.

SAWA: How about it? Do you have any prospects for the older of these two?

ETSUKO: Papa, that's all you ever think about! You really don't have to bring it up right now.

KAMIYA *(laughing)*: I can't hear a word you're saying!

SAWA: Tell me, are you really in such a hurry today? I'm already having our woman prepare dinner.

AIKO *(to Etsuko)*: What shall we do, I wonder?

SAWA: We won't keep you.

KAMIYA: No, no, I'm sorry, but I really can't. It's already time for my appointment. Etsuko, next time, please allow me to take you and Aiko somewhere, will you? A Sunday would be good.

AIKO *(to Kamiya)*: The phone's not in my office, so they'll have to come and get me, but if you'd call me. . . . *(So saying, she takes a calling card from her purse and hands it to Kamiya.)*

SAWA: When did you have cards made up?

KAMIYA: I hate to have to admit it, but my beloved wife has taken to sifting through my mail looking for letters with women's names on the envelopes. If she finds this. . . .

SAWA: You get letters from women?

KAMIYA: I swear by my conscience in your daughters' presence it's nothing illicit. But the old battle-ax has been saying she'd like to have a daughter like yours.

*Just then, Raku enters with a letter.*

RAKU: Special delivery.

SAWA: Special delivery? *(Taking it from her)*: Tiens! Who could it be from? Let's see, Tadokoro Rikichi? *(His daughters look meaningfully at one another.)*

KAMIYA: Well, I really must be on my way. Ladies.

SAWA: All right, then. We'll make the sukiyaki some other time, I hope?

KAMIYA: By all means. *Bon soir, mon vieux! (He extends his hand.)*

SAWA: *Mes compliments à Madame!*

*Everyone goes to the entrance to see Kamiya off.*

*Shortly, Etsuko and Aiko return.*

ETSUKO: They're the same type, aren't they?

AIKO: Perhaps, but there's a difference. There's something repulsive about him.

ETSUKO: Do you think so? He seems more harebrained than Father, but. . . .

AIKO: Especially the the way he thinks he's got it all figured out.

SAWA *(entering)*: Interesting fellow, but he lacks tact. It's men like him who succeed, though, so you can see there's room out there for all kinds.

AIKO: Papa?

SAWA: I know. I'll give it to you in a minute. I'm a little concerned about this letter. I haven't the faintest idea who this Tadokoro Rikichi is. *(He opens the letter.)*

ETSUKO: Oh, don't you remember?

AIKO: He's one of the friends Hatsuo brought home last summer.

SAWA *(after reading in silence for a few moments)*: Yes, I see, that's what he says. He says he was on the same ship as Hatsuo. "I have wanted to describe to you your son's last hours, because, as one of his compatriots who, though the task proved too much for him, remained at his bedside and attempted to provide comfort until the end, I have long felt it was my duty to do so. In addition, although Hatsuo is no longer with us, I would like to consult you as his father on a personal matter of the utmost urgency." What the hell does he mean by that? "Fortunately, I have just received shore leave, and I would be exceedingly grateful if you could find the time to see me. I hesitate to visit you without prior notice, and so I would appreciate it very much if you could indicate a time when it might be convenient for me to call. You will find my address below. Just in case, my telephone number is Shitaya 1793."

*There is a long silence.*

AIKO: How strange. *(She looks at Etsuko.)*

ETSUKO *(in a small voice)*: I know.

SAWA: "A personal matter of the utmost urgency"? What does he mean he wants to consult me "as Hatsuo's father"?

ETSUKO: He wants you to advise him as Hatsuo would have.

SAWA: I understand that, but what exactly does he want me to advise him about?

AIKO: You had better ignore it. If you start worrying about other people, there'll be no end to it.

SAWA: Let's see, last summer? He was one of the friends Hatsuo brought home, is that it? I can hardly recall his face, but. . . . Didn't you two go off with them someplace?

ETSUKO: You remember, it was a picnic to Okutama.

*Aiko remains silent.*

ETSUKO: We were all completely sunburned by the time we got home, but. . . .

SAWA: Well, I suppose I will have to see him. Why don't the two of you join us?

ETSUKO: We could hear more about Hatsuo, but . . . I don't know. . . .

*(She looks at Aiko.)*

AIKO: Either way's fine with me.   From the way the letter's written, though, I'd say it wouldn't be much fun.

ETSUKO: He really does write in a stodgy old style.   Of course, Hatsuo used to write in the most archaic style, too.   He said that way you didn't have to write so much.

AIKO: Well, let's leave the matter up to Papa.   We should be on our way.

ETSUKO: Wait a minute.   Speaking of Hatsuo, I've begun to recall all sorts of things.   How strange, after all these months!

AIKO: Eternally young, aren't you!

ETSUKO: Early to bed, early to rise,  with chores piled up to here!

AIKO: You'd have your hands full just having a good time.

ETSUKO: That's right!   I usually don't have time to think.   But  tonight, somehow. . . .   I haven't felt this way in so long. . . .   Go ahead and laugh if you like, but I think I'd like to savor this feeling for a while.

AIKO: Right now?   Come on, do me a favor!

ETSUKO *(going to her father)*:  Papa, don't you think it's sad when there are  secrets  between  brothers  and sisters or parents and children? Maybe I shouldn't say "secrets," but isn't it awful when you have to suffer with something alone?

SAWA: Why do you say that all of a sudden?

ETSUKO:  No reason, really.   I was just thinking about Hatsuo, and I began to wonder if families aren't supposed to be closer than we are. We've all been leading our separate lives.   There's too much we don't know about each other.   In our family, nobody ever shares anything. Why is that?

AIKO: Because we can't rely on each other, that's why.   Do  you want  to know the solution to the world's problems?   Courage, money, and time--in that order.   Personal ambition and sympathy won't get you anywhere.

ETSUKO: But that's what  I mean.   What do you do when you're out of courage and money and time?

AIKO: We're not talking about catching a train--there's always time.

ETSUKO: Until you die, anyway.

SAWA: Let me see, where did I put Hatsuo's picture?

ETSUKO: Aiko, we can argue anytime,  but for today let's promise.   Henceforth we'll  share all our worries; we won't keep secrets; and we won't hesitate to make demands on one another.

AIKO: Etsuko, are you against taking responsibility for your own actions? I don't want to argue with you; I'm just asking.

ETSUKO: I don't think there's any contradiction between taking responsibility for your own actions and what I just said.

SAWA:  All right.  I see what both of you mean.  You're both right.  I'll offer a compromise.

AIKO:  Go ahead.  After all, there's no point in making promises you can't keep.

ETSUKO:  There was too much of the schoolmarm in the way I put it, wasn't there?  How can I say it better?  I guess I'm feeling that we're growing apart, and that makes me lonely.  If we don't embrace each other now while we still can, where will we end up?

AIKO:  Papa, when we were  children,  which of us did you prefer?

SAWA *(laughing uncomfortably)*:  Well, let me see. . . .

ETSUKO:  You, of course.  You were in his arms from the moment you were born.

*Sawa evades the issue with a laugh.*

AIKO:  Is that really such a hard thing to admit?

SAWA:  In any case, I  was out of the country by the time you were four and your sister was six, so. . . .

AIKO:  Come on, admit that you liked me better.

ETSUKO:  You can even tell by her name: Aiko--"Child of Love."

SAWA:  Come now, that's. . . .

AIKO:  I'm not saying it has anything to do with the present.  I'm talking about before, in the past.  Ah, I'm so happy!  That's one of Papa's great secrets, you know.

ETSUKO:  Stop it now.  You're torturing him.

SAWA:  If you're going to dredge that up. . . .  Oh, never mind, I guess I'll let  you get away with  it.  Your mother knows the truth.  Once, I walked back and forth on the  veranda with you in my arms and Etsuko on my back, singing "The Whistle Blew."

ETSUKO:  What did you do that for?

SAWA:  To get you to sleep, of course.  You were both terrible cry babies.

ETSUKO:  What was Mother doing?

SAWA:  Hm, I really don't know.

AIKO:  I do.  She'd left you and gone back to Grandma and Grandpa.

SAWA:  So you know about that.

*Pause.*

ETSUKO:  Remember when Hatsuo brought a bunch of his school friends home and shouted, "Hey, anybody want a sister?  You can have mine for nothing!"  How old was I?  He'd called me out in front of them, and  I was standing  there oblivious to  what was happening.  Well, not completely oblivious.  It's frightening to think back on your childhood.

AIKO: When you're finished, let's go.  I've got things to do tonight.

*Just then, Raku enters to clear off the table.*

RAKU: You must be hungry.

ETSUKO: Not really.  Dinner's not  ready yet, is it?  We were just leaving.

RAKU: Oh!

AIKO: You don't have to act so surprised.  We planned to eat out anyway.

*Sawa clears his throat meaningfully.  Raku exits.*

SAWA: I've completely lost my taste for European food lately.  You girls
are always clamoring for Western cuisine.  I don't know what you see
in the stuff.

ETSUKO: Well, it works out fine, then, doesn't it?  Raku says the smell
of butter makes her sick to her stomach anyway.

SAWA: Etsuko, go upstairs and bring me my suit coat.  No, never  mind.
You wouldn't know where it is.  I'll go.  *(He exits.)*

AIKO: That letter.  Do you think Papa really doesn't remember?

ETSUKO: *I* do.

AIKO: Please, Etsuko, do me a favor and stay out of this, all right?

*Sawa returns,  tosses a wad of bills onto the table, and non-chalantly
lights a cigarette.*

AIKO *(sliding the money toward her, to Etsuko)*: I'll take this, and that
will make us even.  That's all right with you, isn't it?

ETSUKO *(laughing)*: I suppose it'll have to  be.  I'll borrow some more
when I need it.  Papa,  Aiko says she's going to buy this marvelous
piano.  From Germany.

SAWA: Where did you get that kind of money?

AIKO: I found a really inexpensive old thing.  Secondhand, of course.  It
only costs 400 yen.

SAWA: That's what I mean: where did you come up with the money?

AIKO: Why, the bank, of course.

ETSUKO:  Don't you know, Papa?  Aiko's a regular woman of means!
*ing at her sister)*: May I tell him?

AIKO: It's nobody's business how much a person's got in the bank.  Oh,
by the way, Papa, you  don't mind if I take this doll, do you?  I've
been wanting it for the longest time.  *(She picks up the Dutch doll on
the shelf.)*

ETSUKO: No fair!

SAWA: That doll. . . . .  Well, all right.  But don't give it away, do you
understand?

AIKO *(shouting into the interior of the house)*: Raku!  Raku!  Did you change the light bulb in my room? *From the interior, Raku's voice replies, "I'll do it right away."*

ETSUKO: Change your own light bulbs.

*Shortly, Raku appears with a light bulb. Aiko grabs it from her and holds it up to the light.*

AIKO: This won't do, it's only sixteen candle power. It has to be thirty-two or I can't see to read.

*Sawa has been listening with irritation to his daughter's disrespectful language. For a while he controls himself, his eyes closed.*

SAWA *(finally)*: Aiko--and you, too, Etsuko--there's something I've been meaning to tell you. *(Long pause.)* Raku isn't just an employee anymore.

*Each of the women is shocked in her own way by this unexpected announcement. They acknowledge each other warily as they draw back, almost cowering.*

SAWA: I don't know whether I'll have you call her "Mother" or not. You probably have your own opinions on the subject. I just realized that this isn't the sort of thing to keep under wraps. You two don't have to worry about anything--you can just go ahead and build your lives, carefree as before. Raku's spent half her life unhappy. And I was weak. It must have been meant to happen. Don't say anything; just act as if nothing has changed.

*As if on cue, Raku and Etsuko cast their eyes downward. Aiko alone stares defiantly at her father.*

*Curtain.*

## ACT TWO

*The scene is the same as Act One. It is ten o'clock on a Sunday morning several days later.*

*Sawa and Tadokoro Rikichi (29) are sitting opposite each other at the table. Tadokoro wears a second mate's uniform and an insistent smile on his ruddy face.*

TADOKORO: If we'd been near Hong Kong or Hawaii, there would have been good hospitals in the area, and things might not have had to turn out as they did. Hatsuo just got sick at the wrong time.

SAWA: I'm sure you did everything you could for him, and I'm grateful. He just didn't take very good care of himself, and it caught up with him. I don't think he drank much, but he was a fool when it came to food.

TADOKORO: But Hatsuo was still more conservative than some. Take that fellow Okada who was with us last summer. . . .

*Etsuko appears.*

ETSUKO: Aiko says she's not feeling well and asks to be excused. She seems to be catching a cold.

TADOKORO (*standing and looking inquiringly into Etsuko's eyes*): Couldn't she just come down for a minute?

SAWA: Yes, she was up for breakfast this morning.

ETSUKO: She is up. I guess she doesn't want to see you looking as she does. By the way, how is Mr. Okada?

TADOKORO: As always. We were just talking about him. The fellow found himself a wife last summer. . . .

ETSUKO: Oh!

TADOKORO: It's really a laugh. Every time he goes ashore, he goes home to his wife, naturally--that's to be expected--but when he returns to the ship, he always has the runs! Apparently he has his wife fix him sweet bean soup with dumplings, and he eats it till it makes him sick!

ETSUKO: My word!

TADOKORO: Sailors are just like children.

ETSUKO: For a child, he certainly drank a lot of beer that time.

TADOKORO: That was Hatsuo's fault. He was a master at egging people on, a regular firebrand. Did you hear about the time he got our captain into bed with a nigger woman? Oops, sorry!

SAWA: With what?

ETSUKO: That's disgusting! With a nigger woman, he said.

SAWA: You did?

TADOKORO: Not me. Please forget I mentioned it. I guess my head comes a little unscrewed when I'm on dry land. Sorry.

SAWA: Let's see now, I believe there was something you wanted to discuss with me. Do you mind if Etsuko is present?

ETSUKO: I was just about to excuse myself. I have to prepare my lessons for tomorrow. Please, make yourself at home.

*For a while after Etsuko has left, the two men sit in silence, smoking their cigarettes.*

TADOKORO: I don't know exactly how to begin.

SAWA: Don't stand on ceremony, son, just spit it out. Whether I'll be able to help or not is another matter, of course.

TADOKORO: That's just the problem. Well, here goes. It's about Aiko.

*Sawa is surprised but silent.*

TADOKORO: I've finally got my chief mate's credentials, and so it's about time to. . . .

SAWA: Say no more. I understand. You want my permission to marry Aiko. Well, you won't get very far discussing the matter with me. You'd think that I could at least relay the message, but as a father, I have certain responsibilities. Aiko says that she'll handle her own affairs. Of course, she's a bright young woman, and I trust her completely, so I've given her *carte blanche* to do as she pleases. The parents of the world have a tendency to want to intervene in their daughters' future, but how successful are they in making their daughters happy? In that respect, I think I have a pretty accurate understanding of a parent's limitations. It would be different if it were Aiko asking my advice--I could offer her some inoffensive platitudes--but both my daughters, particularly Aiko, have minds of their own. Even if I were in a position to bring the subject up, she wouldn't listen to me. So it looks like you're on your own.

TADOKORO: If that's the way you feel, I don't know what I'll do. I don't have anyone left to turn to. I should have told you this before, but actually, before he died, I had Hatsuo ask Aiko how she felt toward me.

SAWA: And?

TADOKORO: Of course it was by letter, but the answer was totally unexpected, and I only became more confused about Aiko's real feelings.  To make a long story short, in her words, "I don't remember anyone named Tadokoro, and consequently I have no interest in him whatsoever.  In any event, I have no intention of marrying, and therefore I would like to end any further discussion of the subject at this point."

SAWA:  She said she doesn't intend to get married?  That's news to me, too.  But if that's the case, you had best reconcile yourself to the fact.

TADOKORO:  No, whether she marries or not is beside the point.  I just can't believe that she's forgotten me.  We spent two full days face to face like that,  after all.  After we spent a day together here at your home, we all went on a picnic up to Okutama.  On the way, we horsed around and really got to know each other.

SAWA:  Perhaps she's got you confused with Mr. Okada.  You're both so dark, maybe she couldn't tell the difference.

TADOKORO:  In any case,  the whole thing would be cleared up if I could just see her, but the way things are going today, that seems out of the question, so I'll come back again some other time.  The only  thing is, I don't want there to be any misunderstanding about  my visit today.  If she says she doesn't want to see me, I won't make an issue of it,  but I'd at least like to know why.

SAWA:  Now wait just a minute.  Something bothers me.  Judging from the way you talk, it sounds as if you think Aiko knows your intentions and is refusing  to see you on purpose.  In that case, there shouldn't be any need for you to hear her answer.

TADOKORO:  It's not so  much her answer as her reason  that I want to hear.

SAWA:  Reason for what?

TADOKORO:  The reason she can't answer.

SAWA:  You haven't even asked her yet whether she can answer you or not.

TADOKORO:  Don't you understand?  As I said before, her answer to Hatsuo was no answer at all.

SAWA:  Or it might have been in lieu of an answer.

TADOKORO:  The reason you say that is because you don't know the most  important point.  You think ours is just a casual relationship.

SAWA:  That's an alarming thing to say.  What sort of relationship do men and women have if it isn't "casual"?

TADOKORO:  Ask Aiko to come down here and you'll see.  Let her stand here in front of me.  I think you'll understand immediately.

*For a moment, Sawa stares blankly at his opponent.  Eventually he rises and starts toward the interior of the house.  But he thinks better of it and returns to his seat.*

SAWA: All right, let me speak to Aiko. For the time being, you be on your way. If things are as you say, leave this problem up to me.

TADOKORO: I have no objection to leaving the matter in your hands, but will you let me see Aiko some time soon?

SAWA: If there's a need. If it turns out that it would be better for both parties if you didn't meet, then, well, there'll be no need.

TADOKORO: No, then everything would be decided according to your judgment. I want to hear an unequivocal answer from Aiko's lips in any case.

SAWA: There won't be any need to hear it if the answer is no.

TADOKORO: But please tell her that I won't accept a simple no.

SAWA: What do you mean "won't accept"?

TADOKORO: I mean I won't be satisfied.

SAWA: That's out of the question. I don't know what promises you made, but promises just between the two of you can't be considered binding. In the first place, as Aiko's parent I shouldn't be kept in the dark.

TADOKORO: I thought you said your policy was not to interfere?

SAWA: At the moment it is. But if my daughter is going to be held to that kind of promise and is going to be forced to do something against her will, then I'll see to it that she cancels her promise. I couldn't do otherwise.

TADOKORO: I can see that it's pointless to say anything more at this time. I'll wait for the opportunity to see Aiko. I'll be satisfied if I understand. I have no intention of doing anything dishonorable. But even the most cloistered young lady, no matter how ignorant she may be of the ways of the world, has to take responsibility for her own actions, that's all. I'd like her to act in such a way that the other person involved can at least walk away with his pride intact. Even if we are to put the past behind us, there must still be any number of ways for her to make her present position clear.

SAWA: You keep talking about the past, so while you're at it, why don't you tell me about it. Exactly how far did your relationship go?

TADOKORO: In order for me to tell you that, I would have to have Aiko's consent. May I have it?

SAWA: I suppose. . . . No, wait. If you have that much consideration for Aiko's feelings, then I won't inquire further. I'll get the story directly from Aiko. There's no need to put this off to another time. You stay here and talk to Etsuko while I look in on Aiko.

*As Sawa exits, Etsuko enters in his place.*

ETSUKO *(softly)*: Why is Aiko being this way? I wonder if she's embarrassed to see you? I know about the letter.

TADOKORO: Oh, you mean my letter? Did she really tear it up without reading it? That's what she told Hatsuo. I can't believe it.

ETSUKO: Nor can I. It's so strange, because she's hiding her relationship with you. I was just talking to her in her room, and there's something very strange going on with her. She probably really isn't feeling well, but there's no reason why she can't at least say hello. I don't know how many times I told her that. But it was no use. She's changed. She's colder or stronger, I don't know, but compared to before, she's lost her femininity. She seems to want to be that way. But in terms of her feelings toward you, there is something unnatural going on. I don't know exactly what, but. . . .

TADOKORO: I just described the situation to your father, but it's so hard to explain when you're only telling one side of the story.

ETSUKO *(her eyes widening with curiosity)*: Oh my! Do you mean there's so much to explain? You can't be serious! After all, you were only together for two days!

TADOKORO: Two days or not, what happened happened.

ETSUKO: Yes, I suppose it did. But in that case, she really. . . . There must be some reason why she won't see you.

TADOKORO: That's what I think, too.

ETSUKO: I see. . . . I thought you were still just exchanging letters. But there's more between you than that, isn't there?

TADOKORO: Come on, you of all people. . . .

ETSUKO: But I want to know. Don't be so evasive. Tell me, where did it happen? When?

TADOKORO: Those aren't things one divulges so easily.

ETSUKO: That's strange! You mean there's something you can't talk about? I tell you, you can't take your eyes off that girl for a minute. *(As if searching her mind for something)*: Let's see, that night we all stayed in that filthy inn, whatever it was called, in Okutama. You all got drunk.

TADOKORO: Not me particularly.

ETSUKO: You were singing till all hours, all by yourself.

TADOKORO: I wasn't sleepy.

ETSUKO: I didn't notice anything special right up to the time we returned home.

TADOKORO: In me?

ETSUKO: In either of you.

TADOKORO: There's the problem right there. We never did speak to each other after that. As we were parting at Tokyo Station, I wanted to say something, but she wouldn't look at me. No, it was that way from the moment we left the inn. When our eyes met, she'd look away, and when I tried to talk to her, she'd find some excuse to run on ahead. In the train, no matter how many times I tried to speak to her, she pretended she couldn't hear me. It was terrible.

ETSUKO: How could I have been so blind? I didn't notice a thing! But what could she have been thinking? She's not the talkative type, so. . . .

TADOKORO: She was talkative enough on the way out. She joined in the fun with everyone else. In fact, the whole thing began when she powdered my nose with her compact.

ETSUKO: I remember that. We were trying to decide which of you three men had the darkest complexion.

TADOKORO: Aiko had been totally absorbed in her make-up, so I was startled when she shouted, "This one!" and reached out for me, sitting beside her.

ETSUKO (*accepting this explanation*): So that's how it began?

TADOKORO: I think so.

ETSUKO: It's really strange, how that sort of thing excites men.

*Tadokoro forces a smile.*

ETSUKO: I don't want to sound jealous, but Aiko's a lot bolder than I am.

TADOKORO: Of course you're the first one people feel attracted to. Okada said the same thing--how he'd like a big sister like you.

ETSUKO: Big sister! Am I such an old woman?

TADOKORO: People forget their age and turn into children when they're with you. It's that way from the first moment. I was pretty excited before, but when I saw you, I just sort of withered.

ETSUKO: Withered?

TADOKORO: It's a way of saying I felt like surrendering without a fight.

ETSUKO: Shall I make some tea? (*She touches the teapot on the table.*) This seems a little cold.

*Pause.*

TADOKORO: Are you still at that school?

ETSUKO: I still have a little time before I retire.

TADOKORO: That's not what I mean. Does the work still interest you?

ETSUKO: There might be something more suited to my personality than teaching, but working in that school keeps me from indulging myself, and that makes it all worthwhile. I can't think of another situation where I'd be less likely to develop a craving for worldly pleasures. I don't go around each day visiting the homes of poor children out of a feeling of superiority. I'm not like those do-gooders who devote themselves to the poor only so long as it doesn't affect their wallets. Everything I have goes into my work. I'd rather spend a penny for the starving than on myself. Without giving any fancy reasons, it's simply what makes life worth living right now.

TADOKORO: It's a rosy world you live in, isn't it?

ETSUKO: No, quite transparent, actually. I detest doing things in the name of Society or Religion. I don't even want to fly the banner of Humanitarianism.

TADOKORO: You were just born this way?

ETSUKO: Sentimental, you mean? I wouldn't complain if I had been. I'm the headstrong type, anyway. The gloomy world I grew up in as a child must be responsible. I can't forget the degradation I felt at school when we children compared the contents of our lunch boxes.

TADOKORO: Hatsuo used to talk a lot about the same thing. This was while your father was away, wasn't it? Even so, it's hard to imagine siblings more different than you three.

ETSUKO: Hatsuo was the carefree one.

TADOKORO: I don't know whether he was carefree or just plain dumb, but he'd do the wildest things without thinking twice. This is just between you and me, but once he stuffed a coolie who'd been stealing on board ship into a gunny sack and dumped him into the sea.

ETSUKO: What happened?

*Just then, Sawa reappears.*

SAWA: It's hard to figure out what happened listening to the two of you separately, but. . . . *(Noticing Etsuko)*: Etsuko, it might be best if you excused yourself. *(He waits until she has left the room.)* What you said before seems to be true. Aiko hasn't forgotten you. She's taken back what she said, so you can relax on that score. On the other hand, she insists that she never promised you anything. Perhaps you misunderstood. Or maybe you just imagined it?

TADOKORO *(forcing a smile)*: If so, that makes me look pretty stupid, but at this point I'm reluctant to say anything more about the facts. I'm reluctant for the sake of my own self-respect. Nevertheless, I would like you to ascertain why, in your fair judgment, Aiko refuses to see me.

SAWA: She says that she won't see you because she doesn't want to. That may not be any way to treat a gentleman, but I suppose it's reason enough for a spoiled girl like Aiko. Of course, that makes my position as her father rather awkward. But let me beg your indulgence for my inadequacy, and ask you to let Aiko get away with this selfishness for the time being. They say human beings are creatures of emotion, and that's especially true of women. Look, show your mettle as a man and consider the fact that Aiko would even make the excuse that she doesn't feel well as an endearing idiosyncrasy.

TADOKORO: There's no reason why I should understand female psychology so profoundly, but I do know that it can't be dismissed simply by saying it's unfathomable. If Aiko is simply going to refuse to recognize the facts, I can accept that. But as a last favor, I'd like to hear it directly from her. Would that be all right?

SAWA: As I just said. . . . Look, she may be twenty-four, but women are still children at that age. They can't stand on their own two feet. They can't think up a gentle way to refuse a man they know is after them. So they say they don't feel well or develop cramps or whatever else pops into their head.

TADOKORO: I don't want her to turn me down gently. If she dislikes me, fine. I just want to know why she feels she has to tease me this way, as if I were a craven sneak-thief. I'd like to know why, if she doesn't want to see me, if she doesn't care for me anymore, she can't just come right out and say so. Otherwise, how can I forget her? There's something wrong with the whole lot of you!

SAWA: Keep your voice down. The neighbors will hear. We're not in the middle of the Indian Ocean, you know.

TADOKORO: If this were the middle of the Indian Ocean, you'd all be dead!

*In a rage, he kicks away his chair and starts to exit.*

*Sawa hastily tries to intercept him, but when he realizes that he is heading out of the house, he shows relief and simply watches him go.*

*A few moments pass, then Raku enters timorously. She begins to clear the tea cups from the table.*

RAKU: What shall I do about lunch?

SAWA (*without looking at her, after a few moments of silence*): Did you hear?

RAKU: No . . . well, some. . . .

SAWA: I'll have noodles again. Go see what that Aiko is up to. If she's acting as if nothing happened, tell her I want to see her.

*Etsuko enters as Raku exits.*

ETSUKO: So he finally left. I was afraid he might do something.

SAWA: Did you hear his story? Damned fool story!

ETSUKO: If he's acting like a fool, Aiko's probably to blame.

SAWA:  Whoever is to blame, I'm the one who looks foolish.  It's a strange business.  I still don't know whether I understand it or not.  Has Aiko said anything to you?

ETSUKO:  Putting both their stories together, I think I have a pretty good idea what happened.

SAWA:  I do, too.  Aiko probably let him hold her hand or something of the sort.

ETSUKO:  I wonder.  He wouldn't have gotten so upset if that were all there was to it.

SAWA:  Maybe.

ETSUKO:  Ah-ah!  People are so strange!

SAWA:  One way or another, I'll get the truth out of Aiko.

*Aiko enters, looking as if nothing has happened.*

AIKO:  Oh!  Etsuko, are you here?

ETSUKO:  Should I go in the other room?

AIKO:  Why?  I don't mind.  Papa, did you want to see me?

SAWA:  Yes.  Have a seat.  Tell me, exactly how do you feel about this fellow Tadokoro?

AIKO:  I don't feel anything at all about him particularly.  I just think he's a nuisance.

SAWA:  A man has to have some reason to make such a stink.  As I told you before, you must have done something to lead him on.  You may claim to know nothing about it, but he says that he has proof.  I didn't ask him for it, and he wouldn't come right out and say it, but I had the feeling that he had the advantage.  I didn't think there was any cause to force you to see him against your will, so I got rid of him, but now you owe me an explanation.  If I go out on a limb for you, I don't want to have it cut off.  That's what I'm worried about.  The fellow seems discrete enough, for a sailor, and ingenuous considering his age.  There must be some way to make him understand that the past is the past and things are different now.  If you're willing to deal with the problem on that basis, I'd be willing to make allowances.  But you can't just claim that you don't know anything about it.

*Silence.*

ETSUKO:  I suppose this is no time for me to stick my nose in, but that's just what I said the other day.  It's a pity to suffer with something like this all alone.

SAWA:  Etsuko, perhaps you'd better leave the room after all.

*After Etsuko has whispered something more in Aiko's ear, she leaves the room with a strange air of self-satisfaction.*

SAWA:  All right, if you can think of something you did that might have given this fellow the wrong impression, let's hear it.

*Aiko does not respond.*

SAWA: Isn't there anything you did that might have excited him unintentionally?

AIKO *(curtly)*: There must have been any number of things like that.

SAWA: There were? I see. All right, let's hear them, one at a time.

AIKO *(still with detachment, as if she were talking about someone else)*: First, when we picked up our tickets in Shinjuku--he'd bought tickets for everybody--in the process of taking my ticket from him I clutched his fingers. When I looked up in surprise, he was blushing and kept on bowing over and over again.

SAWA *(considering)*: I see. And then?

AIKO: When we were getting off the train, he tried to get the lunch boxes down from the overhead rack all by himself, so without thinking anything of it, I helped him by taking them from him one by one. Well, he apologized every time he handed me a box, so I just said there was nothing to be sorry for. That's all. Then he got this tearful look on his face and began staring into my eyes.

SAWA *(considering)*: I see. That's all there was to that, is that right?

AIKO: Yes. Then when we got on the Ōme train, there was almost no one else in the car, so everyone began horsing around. One minute they'd be singing songs, and the next they'd be insulting each other. It was a regular riot. I was just sitting there listening, but then Hatsuo invented this childish game where one person would toss out a problem--Who's got the worst complexion?--and the other four would all try answering at once. Who's the most stuck-up? Etsuko thought up that one. Anyway, Hatsuo and Mr. Okada shouted, "Tadonkoron!"--that's his nickname--and right away he said, "The person next to me!" That was me. But the majority rules, so he lost. Next, I think it was Mr. Okada who said, "The darkest one!" I had just taken out my compact, so when I tried to say "This one!" and point, I wound up touching his nose.

SAWA *(considering)*: And you got powder on him. *(A long silence.)* And the rest are all the same sort of thing? There wasn't anything more serious?

AIKO: All right, I'll make a clean breast of it. You remember everybody got drunk, and we decided to stay overnight in an inn. The three men and two women slept in separate rooms, of course. Before long, you could hear the sound of snoring coming from the men's room. But that fellow stayed awake and kept singing until all hours. It wasn't particularly loud, but the melody was plain enough.

SAWA: He wasn't talking in his sleep?

AIKO: No. Etsuko had pulled the covers over her head, so you couldn't tell which end was up. I can't sleep that way, so I was left wide awake under the light. You could hear the sound of the stream outside, and when his bass blended with it, it turned into the kind of quiet night when you're afraid to turn over in bed.

SAWA: Were the sliding doors between your rooms closed?

AIKO: That's just it. They were closed, but not all the way. That bothered me, so without thinking I stuck out my hand to try to close them. Someone grabbed my hand, and I was blind with fear. My voice had left me, too. When I regained my composure, I realized that the room was black as pitch. A wind had come up outside. The shutters were making a terrible racket.

SAWA: You knew for sure it was him?

AIKO *(suddenly on the offensive)*: What if I did? So what? *(Vehemently)*: I can't stand it! It doesn't amount to anything. It's the same as if nothing happened. There isn't a woman in the world stupid enough to commit herself to a man because of a thing like that. What does it prove? What does he think he's won from me? Let him gloat if he wants. He talks about promises. What did I promise him? If he thinks it's proof I love him, he's got another think coming. So, you see! Now you probably want to know why I didn't refuse him. Well, Papa, women just aren't that simple! *(She buries her face in her arms on the table.)*

*At this point Etsuko appears at the entrance. She shoots a meaningful glance and a smile of satisfaction at her father. Instead of responding, Sawa quietly closes his eyes.*

ETSUKO *(gently placing her hand on Aiko's shoulder)*: It's all right. It's all right, Aiko. We're on your side. You must have suffered with this for a long time. Poor thing. If I'd known you had a secret like this, I'd have tried to be more sympathetic. You've been so distant from us, and now all of a sudden we're close again. It's almost like a dream. I don't know whether to be happy or sad. If the past has to be buried, so be it--let's bury it quickly. Are you still crying?

AIKO *(raising her head suddenly)*: No, I'm not crying. *(And in fact she is not.)*

ETSUKO: Here, come closer to me.

AIKO: Thank you, but no. It's a lie we've grown closer, a big lie.

ETSUKO: Why do you say that?

AIKO *(coldly)*: Papa, as of today, I'm leaving this house. Don't worry about me. A lot of things have become clear to me. I see that my life isn't here with you and Etsuko. *(Standing at the entrance and looking back)*: When I know where I'm living, I'll let you know.

SAWA: Aiko! Aiko!

*Aiko disappears.*

*For a while, Etsuko looks after her, but then she notices the tears in her father's eyes and quickly takes out a handkerchief for herself as well.*

*Curtain.*

## ACT THREE

*A room in a boardinghouse. Upstage is a door. To the right is a window.*
*To the left is an alcove with a curtain drawn across it. One end of a bed is*
*visible. In the center of the room is a porcelain brazier for heating.*
*Two years have passed since the last act. It is close to noon on a*
*winter day.*
*A knock at the door. The unshaven man who rises heavily from the*
*bed is Sawa Kazuhisa. He goes to open the door. On the other side*
*stands Okui Raku.*

SAWA: What do you want!

RAKU: Don't snap. Can't I come in?

SAWA: Just hurry up and tell me what you want.

RAKU: You're going to catch a cold like this. Is that all right?

*Sawa grudgingly turns back into the room.*

SAWA *(putting his arms through the sleeves of a quilted robe)*: My
daughters are coming today. I just don't want them to find you here.

RAKU: Then I won't stay long. *(She kneels beside the brazier as she says*
*this.)*

SAWA: Now listen here, in my present circumstances, I can't be giving
you money all the time. I've given up trying to find a position.
Kamiya won't have anything to do with me, and lately I've resigned
myself to the idea that at my age it might be better to lead a frugal
existence than to go around bowing and scraping.

RAKU: Couldn't Aiko do something for you?

SAWA: At least spare me that. Every time she comes, she tries to leave
me something, but I absolutely refuse to accept it. I don't want anything from a woman who'd stoop to marrying a foreigner in order to
live on easy street. She may be my daughter, but I won't compromise my principles.

RAKU: If it were only me, I'd be able to make ends meet on what I'm
getting now, but it's out of the question if I want to send Momoe to
school. I'll apologize personally to Etsuko, so couldn't we please go
back to the way things were?

SAWA: The way things were? You mean the three of us living together?
No thanks. Think of how much I suffered, caught between you and

Etsuko. I wouldn't mind if it were for some other reason, but if she were to threaten to walk out because of you, you know I wouldn't be able to tell her to go to hell. The three of us may have wound up living apart like this because of our damned foolish pride, but at least I've saved face toward the two of you. Let it be. We don't have to change anything. Just leave well enough alone.

RAKU: Just so it's understood that when I came into your house in the first place, I had no idea things would develop as they did.

SAWA: What's the point of saying that now?

RAKU: No point. I'm just saying that I don't know myself what got into me, that's all. Today's the same way: I wandered over here for no particular reason after I had a fall-down-drag-out battle with Momoe over her tuition.

SAWA: If you didn't have any particular reason, you should have had more consideration and gone someplace else. I can't spare two yen, much less five.

RAKU: So, today's the day your daughters are coming?

SAWA: Just remember the third Sunday of the month. It's the day Aiko's husband plays golf. Today there's no wind. It's a perfect day for golf. (*He pretends to swing a club.*)

RAKU: Have you ever played this "golf"?

SAWA (*embarrassed*): Not exactly.

*There is a knock at the door. Sawa, flustered, opens it slightly. A voice says, "There's a phone call for you. From Yokohama."*

SAWA: Thank you. (*To Raku*): Well, I guess you'll be on your way home now?

RAKU: Do I have a choice? (*She gets to her feet and exits with him, but then, as if she remembering*): While I'm here I might as well take your laundry with me again.

*She pulls soiled shirts, underpants, and handkerchiefs from the cupboard and wraps them in newspaper. She puts the suit that lies crumpled on the floor on a hanger and hangs it from a molding on the wall. She empties the pockets and examines their contents. Several silver coins spill from the pocket of the vest. She quickly stuffs one or two into the sash of her kimono.*

*Sawa returns, shivering with the cold.*

RAKU: Oh, by the way, I heard something interesting.

SAWA (*exaggeratedly*): Good news, eh? How nice for a change!

RAKU: I don't know whether it's good news exactly. One of the wholesalers who serves the shop on the first floor of the building where I'm living also supplies stationery to the school where Etsuko works. He was the one who said so--how Etsuko's really something.

SAWA: You should only believe half of what you hear.

RAKU: You're right, it's only a rumor; there may be no truth to it, but apparently she's really something.

SAWA: You keep saying that. She's "really something" what?

RAKU: She's really something despite appearances.

SAWA: What did she do, twist the principal around her little finger or something?

RAKU: I guess it would be better if you didn't hear it from me.

SAWA: Here we go again! Is that a habit of yours too? For the past forty years, every woman I've known has been like this!

RAKU: Then do you want me to tell you?

SAWA: Forget it. I don't want to hear.

RAKU: You're not angry, are you?

SAWA *(blowing on the coals in the brazier)*: I wish I were still young enough to get angry.

RAKU: The way I hear it, Etsuko's got all the young men teachers going crazy over her. The point is, though, that she's been leading them on when in fact she's been going with one of them for three years behind everybody's back. She's apparently a master at keeping things secret. The man's five or six years younger than she is, and when they're at school, she treats him like a child and even sends him out to run errands!

SAWA *(practically putting his face into the brazier and blowing up a cloud of ashes)*: Ouch! *(He looks up at Raku with a grimace)*: Get out of here, will you?

RAKU: All right, all right. If you don't want me for anything more, I'll be on my way.

SAWA: Do as I told you when you say good-bye.

*Raku kisses him awkwardly on the forehead.*

*When she is gone, Sawa begins changing from his kimono into the Western suit. He hums the same melody he sang in the first act. He coughs loudly. He sneezes. He wipes his nose on his hand. As he is trying to button the collar of his shirt, there is a knock at the door.*

SAWA: *Entrez!* Come in!

*Etsuko, her face buried in her wrap, enters.*

ETSUKO: Have things been quiet around here?

SAWA: As death. How about you? Have you had a cold?

ETSUKO: I don't have time to catch a cold. I've been so busy!

SAWA: That's good.

ETSUKO: Is Aiko coming today? *(She helps him on with his vest and jacket.)*

SAWA: She just called. She said that it was time to leave, but the car isn't back from the golf course yet, so she might be a little late. She should be here by noon.

ETSUKO: I especially want to see her today. You know how we left off last time; I felt so badly afterwards. But I guess once you get like that, you can't change. It's just become part of her personality. I don't know how to put it--I guess she just doesn't like the idea of submitting to another person.

SAWA: I'll bet she's not that way with her husband.

ETSUKO: No, she's too good at playing that game. She knows exactly what Europeans see in Japanese women. She knows perfectly well that it would be a mistake to try to act like a European woman just because she's married to a European man. It's really quite impressive actually. The way she plays up to him, for example-- weren't you watching that time? But how is she when she's with us? She changes completely. Why, she's nothing but a geisha! I was shocked when I saw that.

SAWA: There's nothing to be shocked about. When you get married you'll be the same way.

ETSUKO: I will not! I could never perform like this. *(She strikes a pose, snuggling up to him with her head and shoulders.)* I should ask her when she learned to do that.

SAWA: There you go again. You've become a real shrew lately. Look, neither you nor I are in her debt, and each of us has more than enough problems of his own. Look at you, for instance, you're so thin!

ETSUKO: Don't say that! I know I've lost weight. You just watch and see how skinny I get. What do you expect me to do about it?

SAWA: Don't take things so seriously! In life, victory goes to the one who can adapt. Look at Kamiya! The only time he missed a beat was when he married that wife of his. Otherwise, he's just waltzed away from every situation that didn't serve his purposes without giving it a second thought. I found that out the hard way. That's how you have to be. What's wrong? You seem awfully down in the mouth.

ETSUKO: I'd like a glass of water. Do you have any fresh? *(She stops Sawa, who is about to get up.)* Never mind, I'll go out and get some for myself. Lend me a cup, will you? *(She goes to the cupboard and takes out a cup herself.)*

SAWA: I'll go get it for you.

ETSUKO: Really, it's all right. You just stay where you are.
*With heavy footsteps, Etsuko goes into the corridor.*
*Sawa absently watches her go. Then he rises and investigates the contents of his coin purse. The purse contains two or three bills folded into small wads. He sticks two fingers into his vest pocket and tickles out some coins. He thinks for a moment, but he gives no indication that he is aware of anything amiss.*
*The twelve o'clock whistle blows.*
*Etsuko returns. She is very pale.*
ETSUKO: It's so cold!
SAWA: Here, warm yourself by the fire. *(He pulls a chair up next to the brazier.)*
ETSUKO: How is Raku doing these days?
SAWA: What? *(He is pretending not to be able to hear.)*
ETSUKO: Raku! I asked how she's doing these days?
SAWA *(vaguely)*: Oh, she's . . . the same as always.
ETSUKO: It wouldn't bother me a bit if you two got together, you know. Actually, I'd prefer it if you did. In the first place, don't you find it terribly inconvenient to live alone? And in the second, the way things stand, it makes me look like the bad guy. Don't make excuses, just call her here to be with you--as a favor to me.
SAWA: I'm not as badly off as you seem to think. I've gotten used to this life--it's carefree and simple. I can do without a hot breakfast in the morning. If the two of you keep looking in on me like this every so often, I'm satisfied, and this way I'm not a burden to anyone. Say, do you have a fever? You're trembling. *(He places his hand on her forehead.)* Are you still cold?
ETSUKO *(her shoulders heaving as she breathes)*: What's keeping Aiko? Doesn't she know there are people waiting?
SAWA *(rising)*: I'll find out if she's left home yet.
ETSUKO: Are you going to phone? Don't bother. She'll arrive in her own good time. Today I'm going to make up with her once and for all, for the rest of our lives.
SAWA: Won't you need a mediator? I can't help you there any more. After all, you'll be living most of "the rest of your lives" after I'm gone.
ETSUKO: Who needs a mediator! I've figured out a way to handle this by ourselves.
SAWA: That's what you say, but actually you two aren't on such bad terms. I can think of another case far worse. Perhaps I told you this story before, but it's something that happened in the French town of

Tours, where I was first sent by the Foreign Ministry to study the language. It so happened that in the house where I was living there were two women in their fifties. Everyone called one Madame Thépaze and the other Mademoiselle Pauline. They were the elder sisters of the man who owned house. Each paid part of the expenses, and they had a sort of communal living arrange-ment, you see, so apart from the few years when Madame Thépaze was married and living with her husband, the two of them had lived face to face with each other morning and night for their entire lives. Well, you can imagine how surprised I was when I learned that they hadn't spoken to each other for ten years! People said that until they stopped speaking, although they couldn't agree on anything and argued incessantly, at least when they were out with people they still appeared to be just an ordinary pair of sisters. The stories people told about seeing one of them chasing the other out the front gate with a broom actually had considerable charm. But as I say, for the last ten years they had just stopped talking. Of course, they had probably just run out of things to say. But anyway, three times a day I'd find myself in the dining room with them entrenched at opposite ends of the table, refusing to look at each other. Sometimes I felt terrible about it and other times it struck me as funny. I mean, if you carry things to that extreme, you've got a real fight on your hands. They were way past being on bad terms. You'd think if they couldn't stand the sight of each other that one of them would move out, but neither did. That's the interesting thing about foreigners. They fig-ured that the one who moved would be the loser. The wife of the owner, that is, the two ladies' sister-in-law--a splendid, sunny woman--was a good contrast. Which reminds me, the two who were fighting didn't go around scowling all the time. As a matter of fact, when the other one was present, they'd go out of their way to be entertaining. It was a sort of demonstration: "If you think that I'm unhappy just because I'm not speaking to you, you'd better think again!" They'd try to put up a good front, you see. Well, not to be shown up, the other one would grab someone sitting nearby and start regaling him with how happy she's been, how she's been enjoying each day more than the last. And it would go on like that, with one boasting about the trip she's planning with a close friend, and the other bragging about how she was elected to the entertainment com-mittee at the church. It wasn't easy listening to all that, believe me.

*There is a knock at the door.*
SAWA: *Entrez!*

*Aiko enters, dressed elegantly in Western clothes.*

SAWA *(intentionally imitating the inflection of a European gentleman greeting a lady)*: Bienvenue, chère madame! *(Then, as he brings another chair to the brazier)*: Asseyez-vous, Madame la Vicomtesse!

AIKO *(ignoring her father's clownish behavior and turning suddenly to her sister)*: How have you been? Busy?

ETSUKO: Aiko, let's make up today once and for all. It turns out I'll be moving away.

AIKO *(surprised)*: Where?

ETSUKO: I haven't decided exactly yet. As far away as possible, in any case.

AIKO: Why?

ETSUKO: Reasons. I'll explain when we have more time.

SAWA: Are you being transferred?

ETSUKO: Yes, I suppose you might say that.

SAWA: At your request, or? . . .

ETSUKO: Let's talk about that later. What are we going to do today?

SAWA *(looking at Aiko)*: That Chinese restaurant again?

AIKO: Some place with chairs--I couldn't possibly sit on the floor. And in any case, I can't stay long today. I've been invited to tea.

SAWA: Where?

AIKO: The embassy. René will be by to pick me up at two. Won't you leave things to me today?

SAWA: Well, I had put aside a little something to treat the two of you, but there's nothing wrong with being on the receiving end occasionally, I suppose. These are the only clothes I have, though, so. . . . I mean, if it's all right with you, I have no objections.

AIKO: Do you ever clean this room?

SAWA: Listen, I just got up. I still have to make the coffee.

AIKO: Couldn't we do without the coffee? You don't need any, do you, Etsuko?

ETSUKO: But he's so proud of it, let him make us some.

SAWA *(readying the coffee utensils)*: It can only be as good as the ingredients, so I'm afraid it won't be as I'd like.

*While Sawa is busy with the coffee, Aiko approaches the bed and sits down next to her sister. She stares at Etsuko's profile.*

AIKO: You don't look well.

ETSUKO: I'm going to quit the school.

AIKO: Not permanently?

ETSUKO: Actually, there's been some trouble. May I tell you about it?

AIKO: If it's something you want me to hear.

ETSUKO: You haven't changed, have you? Do you remember that time, the time you got so angry and said you were leaving home? You were fuming because you said it was all my fault for taking that fellow's side.

AIKO: Yes, I remember.

ETSUKO: I still don't understand what went wrong. I thought you'd been suffering all alone and tried my best to comfort you, but it had just the opposite effect, and I alienated you, and on top of that we ended up not speaking to each other for all this time. Even now, it seems so strange.

*Aiko is silent.*

ETSUKO: Just before that I'd said we should try not to have secrets from each other. My feelings haven't changed. So now it's my turn to reveal a secret. If your pride was hurt by having that problem aired in front of me, then I suppose you'll have the satisfaction of seeing my pride bruised today. Then we'll be even, won't we? But I'm not as confident in myself as you are, so I'd be happy for any sympathy I could get. Not from just anybody. From you, from my sister. The world seems dark as night for me right now. Perhaps you can't tell me what to do, but I need your strength. Give me a hand when I'm falling. Please, while I still have some hope, point me back in the right direction.

*Aiko remains silent.*

ETSUKO: Will you promise? I won't be able to muster up the courage if you don't reassure me that it won't be in vain.

AIKO: In any case, why don't you tell me about it and see? I'll do whatever I can. Only let me say one thing before you begin. What you think is important may not seem so important to me. In that case, I don't want you complaining that I wasn't as sympathetic as you expected.

SAWA *(pouring coffee into the coffee-server)*: Don't either of you want refills?

AIKO: I'm fine. *(To Etsuko)*: All right, tell me.

ETSUKO: You don't make me feel very secure, but here goes. Perhaps it will make you happy.

*Aiko raises her eyebrows slightly.*

ETSUKO: Actually, I've been involved with one of the teachers at the school for the last three years. Of course, we took every precaution not to let anyone else know. For a long time everything was fine.

*Aiko does not react.*

ETSUKO: Beginning last summer, though, for some reason I began to talk frequently with another one of the teachers. There wasn't anything between us, but the first man began to get these strange ideas into his head. At first I just thought how silly it would be if I had to justify myself for something like that. But jealousy is no joke. In the end, he was glaring at me in front of other people, and when we were alone he'd break down and weep. It got to the point where it didn't matter how much I explained. He really began to get on my nerves in the end. Anybody'd have felt like telling him off. The result, though, pulled me in a direction I really hadn't expected. Almost as a prank, I began to get serious about the second man. Looking back, I don't know how I ever had the nerve to do anything so reckless, but what's done is done. For six months I played the two of them off against each other, keeping my new relationship secret from the first man and giving the other one the impression that I was his alone. I don't know whether I was being gutsy or just plain brazen, but I lived as if I didn't have a conscience. The days went by, and I kept thinking I had to do something, but in the end you could say I got what I deserved. They both found out that I was deceiving them. At the same time, word of the affair reached the principal. The day before yesterday I was called to his office. He asked for my resignation. He had trusted me, of course. As a matter of fact, his trust went beyond our working relationship, and at one point I sensed that it had developed into personal affection. I even had the unsettling realization that if I'd been willing. . . . It's ironic that he should have been forced to give me that ultimatum.

SAWA: Here now, how about a little more while it's hot?

ETSUKO: Let me see, where was I? Oh yes, the principal said that if we were discreet in the future, for his part he would be willing to keep the whole affair quiet and transfer all three of us to different schools, but neither of the men would hear of it. The first man said that it was all his fault that things had turned out as they had; that he wanted to let bygones be bygones and to rebuild our life together. The second man had his own ideas on the subject and insisted that if anyone had a right to me it was him. There was no way I could explain what I was thinking. One of them was twenty-five, and the other is already . . . thirty, I think. Anyway, if you lined the two of them up, I know my feelings would lean toward the first one.

AIKO: The younger of the two?

ETSUKO: Yes. But even putting my feelings aside, I wonder if that wouldn't be the right thing in either case?

SAWA (*finishing his coffee*):  I went to all that trouble, and look, it's getting cold!

AIKO (*without saying anything, she goes to his chair and picks up the coffee cup*):  Is that all?

SAWA:  What are the two of you whispering about?

AIKO:  It's just between us.  You don't need to hear.  (*She goes toward her sister.*)

ETSUKO:  Aren't you interested?

AIKO:  So far you've just told me what happened.  Whether it develops into a scandal or not depends entirely on your attitude.

ETSUKO:  What should I do?

AIKO:  I can tell you what I'd do in your situation, but I'm not sure I know how you'll react.

ETSUKO:  I'm already twenty-eight.  I've reached the point of no return for a woman.  Please, consider me now, when I no longer have the courage, the  money, or the time you talked about.  If you want to know the truth, I'm afraid of ending up alone.  (*She wipes away her tears.*)

*Aiko suddenly bursts out laughing.*

ETSUKO (*tensing*):  What are you laughing about?

AIKO:  I'm sorry.  It just struck me as so funny.

ETSUKO:   Go ahead and laugh.  I should have known you would.  A cold-hearted female like you can't understand anything!  From now on you can just forget you had a sister.  If you think you've got everything figured out,  living like the concubine of some foreigner, you've got another thing coming.  Nothing bothers you, does it?  All a man's face means to you is money.  Happiness to you is a fur coat.

SAWA:  Are you two fighting again?  If that's all you come here for once a month, you can find some place else.  I don't have to lend you my room for that!

AIKO:  Etsuko, remember what happened that time?  I had never been so mortified in my life, and even though you comforted me with your words, in your heart you were gloating.  I looked foolish to you, didn't I?  It made you happy to see me being dragged through the mud, didn't it?  So, it's not that I'm not sympathetic--I am.  It's just our ways of being sympathetic.  Some people get intoxicated with the pleasure of comforting others.  That's you.  I suppose there are some people who would be grateful for that kind of sympathy.  But not me.  That's why I won't extend that kind of sympathy to others. Nothing personal.

ETSUKO:  I don't want to hear your reasons.  I shared your pain with all my heart.

AIKO: You shared my pain? So what? If blunders are the source of human unhappiness, then the right way to treat unhappiness is to laugh at it. Of course, that's not why I laughed just now. I just expressed out loud what you felt in your heart. Do you understand? As you said before, now we're even.

SAWA: Oh, haven't you two had enough yet? I'm getting hungry. *(As he says this, he begins pacing about the room. He is waiting, as usual, for the fighting to cease.)*

ETSUKO: Then our accounts are canceled. Since we've come this far, let's go all the way. From now on we'll be complete strangers. I felt lonely at the prospect of being alone because I knew I had a sister. From now on, I'll have no more reason to see you. *(She stands.)* Father, I'll come back some other time soon.

*So saying, Etsuko leaves the room. Sawa and Aiko watch her go.*

SAWA: What's wrong with her? What's she so upset about?

AIKO: She's wants us to kiss and make up in the grand style, you see, so she has to put on this display of pique. Papa, you have to take her side in this, you understand? Well, there's no point in just the two of us going out, so I'll be on my way. I brought this because I thought I'd take the two of you out for lunch. I'll just leave it here. *(She tosses some bills on the table.)*

SAWA *(flustered)*: There you go again! I told you, I don't like that sort of thing. Take it back. Take it back. I don't want to have anything to do with it. Just because you have a little extra pocket money doesn't mean you have to turn into a spendthrift.

AIKO: As you wish. I suppose I could use a new pair of stockings! *(Putting the bills into her handbag)*: Good-bye, then. I'll see you again next month.

*Aiko makes a leisurely exit.*

*Sawa does not watch her go but removes his jacket. He takes a piece of bread and cheese from the cupboard and paces around the room, eating each in turn, as music from the radio underscores the irony of the scene.*

*Curtain.*

# ADORATION

## (1949)

translated by

Richard McKinnon

*Characters:*
    Old Man
    Young Girl
    Daughter

*A black curtain provides a backdrop before which are placed simple
furnishings on stage left and stage right suggesting the interior of two
separate rooms. The center stage represents a street. The action of the
play takes place in these three areas which are alternately illumined by
stage lights.
The first scene takes place in the street. The dark outlines of two per-
sons are observed in the street as the curtain opens.*

OLD MAN: You are all alone now.

YOUNG GIRL: What are you doing there?

OLD MAN: Nothing, just walking, same as you standing there.

YOUNG GIRL: But we weren't just standing. We were waiting for someone.

OLD MAN: I see. There were quite a few of you, but they have all found
someone and have gone away. Why are you still here?

YOUNG GIRL: You know why. Nobody has asked me to go with him.
No, that's not true. There was one person but I didn't want to. He
was sort of fierce looking.

OLD MAN: Well, I don't suppose you would want to go with just anybody. But the rest of you found what they wanted. There is always a
risk involved. I suppose the one you had picked out wasn't interested
in you.

YOUNG GIRL: That's the way it goes, I guess. I'm not so choosy,
though. It all depends on the day.

OLD MAN: Would you object to an old man like me?

YOUNG GIRL: You're joking! Is that what you had in mind? I'd never
have known. I thought it was odd, you walking back and forth out
there. But why did you wait so long? You could at least have picked
someone out and asked. Some girls prefer older men, you know.

OLD MAN: Really? I suppose they'd be in their forties, though.

YOUNG GIRL: How did you know? Yes, there was one in her mid-
forties. She left just a while ago. But I was thinking of someone else.
She's young, only twenty-five.

OLD MAN: Well, that doesn't matter. Just a while ago I was accosted by
two young girls down the street. This was the first time anything like
this had happened to me. I turned, and then I heard one of them say,
"Oh no, he's old." Sure I'm old, but just the same I didn't like the

way it sounded.

YOUNG GIRL: Oh, you shouldn't let that bother you. They had no way of knowing. They probably thought they were wasting their time.

OLD MAN: Sometimes it is a waste of time, but not always.

YOUNG GIRL: Would you like to go with me tonight?

OLD MAN: I don't know how far I can go, but if you don't mind, why not? I have never done this sort of thing before. How much does it cost? I have only 5,000 yen.

YOUNG GIRL: Oh it won't cost that much.

OLD MAN: I have a granddaughter who ran away. When I walk along with you this way, I almost feel I am taking her back home. How old are you?

YOUNG GIRL: Nineteen, and you?

OLD MAN: Well, how old shall I say I am? Are we going to your place?

YOUNG GIRL: Nobody knows about this at home. We can get a room at a hotel down the street. Oh, here it is. Would you wait out here for a minute? You may come in now.

OLD MAN: So this is the place.

YOUNG GIRL: What's so wonderful about it? How about some beer?

OLD MAN: Well, why not.

YOUNG GIRL: Some money, please.

OLD MAN: How much is it?

YOUNG GIRL: I'll pay for the room at the same time.

OLD MAN: Here. Take what you need out of it.

YOUNG GIRL: Here's your change. Would you leave a tip for the lady at the desk?

OLD MAN: Why not take it out of that?

YOUNG GIRL: What do you do for a living?

OLD MAN: You wouldn't understand.

YOUNG GIRL: I see. You would feel embarrassed if others found out what you did for a living.

OLD MAN: Now, you shouldn't talk like that. You look sleepy. Come over here, and put your head down on my lap.

YOUNG GIRL: I'm going to take my clothes off. It's so hot.

OLD MAN: That's far enough, far enough. A cool breeze is coming up. You say you are doing this on the sly. But don't your parents say anything about your staying out night after night?

YOUNG GIRL: Father doesn't live with us and mother almost never comes home at night.

OLD MAN: But don't you have brothers and sisters?

YOUNG GIRL: I have two younger brothers, but it costs a lot to send your brothers to school.

OLD MAN: Aren't your brothers old enough to work?

YOUNG GIRL: I was lying, I have no brothers. I have two sisters. My older sister lost her husband in the war and she does piece-work at a vocational school, I think it is.

OLD MAN: Let's speak the truth if we are going to talk at all. It would be silly otherwise.

YOUNG GIRL: But telling the truth would even be sillier. I am always asked about my family and I always make up stories as I go along. It makes no difference, really.

OLD MAN: Probably so to those who really don't care. What is your name? You don't have to tell me your real name.

YOUNG GIRL: I've got only one name, Hisako.

OLD MAN: Hisako, Hisabo, Chaa-chan. You don't mind how I call you?

YOUNG GIRL: Why should you want to remember my name?

OLD MAN: Because I can always recall the face of a girl when I know her name. I have only a few years left to live, and for me this is an important event meeting you tonight. I don't know why I should be telling you this, but you're the only girl I have ever been able to sit with, free of anxiety. Hisako--that's a sweet, gentle name.

YOUNG GIRL: How about your wife?

OLD MAN: You're turning the tables on me now, are you? That I know wouldn't interest you, at all.

YOUNG GIRL: Let's go to bed.

OLD MAN: You go on ahead. I will finish my beer first.

YOUNG GIRL: Here, take back your money, then. Maybe I ought to keep it.

OLD MAN: Sure, keep it all. Just leave me enough for my car fare home.

YOUNG GIRL: Oh, but that's too much. But since you say so. You wouldn't mind if I buy me a handbag with it? I'll be able to get a real good one.

OLD MAN: Of course not, go right ahead. Buy whatever you want. Now, go on and crawl into bed. Go off to sleep if you like.

YOUNG GIRL: Then good night. Hmmm, maybe I'll buy me a pair of white leather sandals, instead.

OLD MAN: You must have many things you want to buy. But what you really want can't be obtained that easily. Even at my age I still don't know what I most want. No, that's not it. I have a feeling that I do know what I want, but I can't quite put it into words. I have seen it with my own eyes. There were times when I thought I could reach for it, but it wasn't that easy. I tried in vain. You're too young to

understand all this, but you ought to think about it once in a while--
where to find that one thing which one would cherish more than anything else in the world.

YOUNG GIRL: What are you mumbling to yourself? Aren't you going to
bed yet?

OLD MAN: You don't feel like rushing into bed when you know you can
go to bed whenever you wish. Half of the pleasure of being old is to
prolong things, but you must be tired out. You don't have to listen to
me talk. But I'm bothering you. I will stop talking.

YOUNG GIRL: No, it doesn't bother me at all. You have a nice, soothing
voice.

OLD MAN: Well, I am glad to hear that. You know, there was a time in
my younger days when I was crazy about singing. Why, if there had
been singing contests in those days, I might well have jumped at the
chance. It's a wonderful thing, throwing yourself into what you do.
The problem is whether you have persistence. When I was a child I
wanted to become a ship's captain and I read everything I could lay
my hands on that dealt with the sea. But I couldn't get into the
marine academy and just because of that I gave up trying to become a
ship's captain. I wonder why I didn't think of working myself up
from seaman? It's funny, but the thought had never occurred to me at
the time. Then I became deeply interested in singing. The problem
there was to get into the music academy, but this my father wouldn't
allow. Instead, I was made a clerk in an attorney's office, something
I didn't want to be at all. Now, this attorney specialized in criminal
cases and I saw criminals day after day until I was sick of looking at
their faces. I even became convinced that these criminals all bore
some resemblance to me. I was frightened; I began to think that there
was no telling what I might do. Then there was my mother, a terribly
capricious woman, who would come right out and say things on occasion that would make me shudder. Not that she was cruel or anything, but sometimes, and when I least expected it, she would act with
total indifference. She was my mother, after all, and once in a while I
felt like making up to her, but how often was I coldly rebuffed.
Nothing hurt me so much as to see her look at me as if to say, "Who
are you?" You have gone to sleep, I see. How peacefully you sleep.
I never developed a deep affection for my mother. True, she had a
soft spot for her children like most parents do, but somehow I never
was able to bring myself to talk to her as I would to a mother. Why,
I couldn't even ask her about an allowance without putting it in a
roundabout away, with my eyes turned away in the direction of my

father. And when this didn't succeed, I would snitch a few pennies from the sales cash. My father operated a toy shop. I remember it well. I was always envious of other mothers, not because they bought our toys, but because you could tell right away that they were mothers. Oh, how often I glowered at children who would ask for something impossible and then throw a tantrum.

YOUNG GIRL: Don't, don't. I said don't, and I mean it.

OLD MAN: Oh, you're talking in your sleep. I wondered. That reminds me of the time I was caught talking in my sleep. I was working for this attorney, as I said before, and got a day off on New Year's Day. I had nowhere to go, so I went home. That night I happened to talk in my sleep. My mother overheard me and told everybody about it the next morning as if she had learned a deep dark secret. She couldn't have been lying, for the girl she had claimed I had mentioned by name happened to be working at this attorney's office. It would have been all right if she had simply brought it up as a joke, but she was plainly making fun of me, the way she talked. She was vulgar, malicious--it was unbearable. I became convinced that this woman distorted everything she touched, that everything in her hands turned ugly. The girl at the office, Kimie Kurahashi was her name, I still remember, was a pretty girl if not a very sociable one. She was a few years older than I and I know I wasn't really in love with her, although I wouldn't deny that I fancied our relations might lead to something more serious. That was really all there was to it. In fact it was funny I should have even mentioned her in my dream. At any rate, I didn't try to justify myself, but what really upset me was that my mother regarded as utterly absurd the notion that I could have a girl friend. This is what destroyed my youth.

YOUNG GIRL: I said I was sorry, didn't I? I'm not the only one to be blamed.

OLD MAN: Of course, everyone is at fault. Don't you worry about such things. Go on with your sleep. Kimie Kurahashi used to lend me all kinds of books. I couldn't give up my dream to become a singer. I would hum tunes to myself at the office, forgetting that visitors were present. I'd be called to task for it and then do it all over again. Finally I was fired. That was 1904, the year the Russo-Japanese War broke out. I failed my physicals--I wasn't built right, they said--so I escaped being drafted, but I applied for a job with the Army as an unskilled worker and later was hospitalized in Mukden. The fellow in the next bed was Kajimura, a newspaper reporter, and he was to play an important role in my life. He is dead now, but in those days he was widely known as a writer, and after we returned to Japan I used to follow him wherever he went. I listened carefully to what he said, even if I didn't always understand what he meant. It was thanks to him that I opened an agency for newspapers and made out pretty well for a while. But then I made a terrible blunder.

YOUNG GIRL: Who? . . .

OLD MAN: What is it that makes you so unhappy? You don't have to cry. Why not? Go ahead and cry all you want. Now about that blunder--I got married. It was just one of those things. Nothing involved or complicated. I had been thinking about getting married and just at that point someone mentioned this girl and said, "How about it?" She was a whimsical girl with rather charming ways about her that struck my fancy. I inquired to see how she felt about the idea and the reply was that she would consider nobody else. I was completely transported by this. This may sound simple enough, but I felt all mixed up inside. I still couldn't believe that this could have happened to me. At the same time I felt rather proud of myself to think there was something even in me that was attractive. Still I was concerned about being overrated by a girl like that. All these thoughts kept going around and around in my mind. But in happiness as someone once said there is always the danger of losing it. We were formally introduced to each other and she became my bride. But no sooner were we married than she began to make a complete fool of me. She started interfering in every single thing I did, as if she were trying to mold me into a man of her liking. She would criticize me for snoring, she would tell me to take up calligraphy to improve my handwriting; she would tell me that I was being too polite to those who worked under me; she would tell me that she didn't want to have children for another two years, that I shouldn't prop my legs up when I sit, that I should have the hair in my nostrils trimmed. She kept nagging me day after day, ordering me to do this or not to do that. It was just intolerable. I may stop to have a few drinks on my way home, and she would immediately cross-examine me as to where I had been. At first, I told her the truth only to learn that this was the wrong thing to do. The fact that geisha were sometimes known to be present in such places irritated her no end. Well, I couldn't always do things that happened to please my wife, and sometimes she got on my nerves and I would snap back at her. It wasn't unusual for us to go a few days at a time without speaking to each other. But then the third year we were married we had our first child. The child died when it was five. I set to wondering. You look around you and notice any number of wives who behave like wives. Why was it that my wife just didn't feel like a wife to me? She managed everything well and she was familiar with things that women were supposed to know about. I had no complaints on this score. And yet at the crucial moment, all of a sudden she ceased to be my wife. She repeatedly reminded me that it wasn't worth being my wife. But a woman who puts her husband under pressure in the way that she did had no business getting married in the first place. I told her so many times. She insisted that the fault lay with me and not with her. I figured that perhaps she had a point and decided to say no more about it.

YOUNG GIRL: You're so silly. Ha, ha, ha, ha!

OLD MAN: Don't frighten me like that. You sound as if you had been listening in all along. Well, it isn't as though we had been bickering for ten or twenty years. We ate our meals together most of the time like any other husband and wife. If we got a free ticket to the theatre I would urge her to go and send her along to the hair dresser's. I took out life insurance, naming my wife as the beneficiary. It was for a larger amount than we could afford. I watched my language in front of other people. She had a chronic valvular disease of the heart and whenever she had a seizure I took care of her throughout the night. And when we were behind on the laundry I helped her out with it, wringing out the clothes or hanging them up. But there was one thing that completely stumped me. It happened one night when we were invited to a wedding in the neighborhood. I was approaching fifty and my wife--let me see--I believe she was forty-two. Maybe she felt in competition with the bride. At any rate she spent a long time getting all prettied up. I noticed a trace of pink around her eyes. She said she was forced to have a drink, and I, feeling jolly myself, told her it was quite becoming. So we got back from the wedding and the minute we walked into our living room, my wife slumped before the hibachi and just sat there, motionless, her chin resting in her hands. Occasionally she threw a sidelong glance in my direction. There was something very strange about the way she looked at me. I remembered then that on our way back she had suddenly stopped talking. Her response had become half-hearted. Thinking that the best thing to do was to leave her alone I prepared to go to bed. I realized I was a little drunk. After a while she turned the light off and crawled into her bed. I called out to her, but she did not answer. I was provoked but there wasn't a thing I could do about it and I gave up. It was then that she said icily, "In all our married life I have never been truly yours." At first I didn't understand what she was trying to say. What she said I heard distinctly. "What?" was all I could say. I was dumbfounded. She was breathing heavily with her shoulders, with her back turned to me. How ridiculous, I said to myself, but I realized, in fact, how serious the situation was. What had made my wife say things like this? But I still didn't have the courage to ask her plainly what she had found dissatisfying about me. The following year, our second child was born, born after a lapse of nineteen years. Her name was Tsuneko, who will be twenty-three this year. Children have a way of being born at odd moments! When the child was four years old her mother died as if glad to be on her way. I brought my daughter up myself. I'm not trying to make a special point of this. There could have been other ways and if I chose to do it this way it was for my own sake, certainly not for anybody else's.

YOUNG GIRL: You're still talking to yourself. What an awful dream I had.

OLD MAN: I didn't think I was talking loud enough to wake you up. But I guess I did wake you, didn't I?

YOUNG GIRL: Uh, uh. You didn't bother me, at all. Weren't the mice running around in the ceiling? I'm sure that's what woke me up. But aren't you sleepy?

OLD MAN: I'll go to bed when I get sleepy. Don't worry about me; go back to sleep. I feel happy just having you beside me like this. I wonder what you mean to me, anyway. Why are you staying in this room alone with me? Can there be a fate more tragic than this? If you were to let me take liberties with you I would first give up being a human being. I'm not trying to pose as a moralist. Nor am I saying that I have suddenly developed a distaste for such things. As I watch you, you seem to become many things to me. Something that is within you moistens my dry throat like water from a fresh spring. What this is I am not sure yet, but I have a strong feeling that it is one of the things I have been searching for all my life. It is something I could not get from my mother or my wife, or even from my daughter with whom I live. There is something strange and wonderful in you that is gentle and all-forgiving. More than anything else you are a woman. To be sleeping innocently at the side of an old man, a total stranger; to want no more, once you have received what you need. Your whole being appears exalted in its beauty.

YOUNG GIRL: Um, um, um. . . .

OLD MAN: Talking in your sleep again. Well, this would be a good time for me to leave quietly. I wonder how Tsuneko is getting along. I hope she has locked the doors and is in bed by now. No, how to kill time till morning. The police might get after me if they found me roaming the streets at this time of night. I suppose I might as well spend the night here. It will be pleasanter to get home after Tsuneko has left the house. I feel wide awake, I don't see how I can get to sleep. Well, a yawn or two might help. There are mice up there after all. How they do run around. I am reminded of a scene from a movie I saw when I was young. I recall the strange, hard expression of a man sleeping alone on a sofa after putting his girl friend to bed. He was a spirited, young man as I recall. Otherwise I am sure the scene would have seemed all too commonplace to me.

*A long pause.*

YOUNG GIRL: Why are you sleeping over there? I wonder what time it is?

OLD MAN: Ah, that was a wonderful sleep! Why it's light outside already.

YOUNG GIRL: My watch is stopped. It always stops again no matter how often I get it fixed.

OLD MAN: It's still a watch. Mine was an exceptionally fine piece, of a foreign make. But since I don't own it anymore I can't even say it's stopped. I don't really regret what I did with it. But it's a pity I can't turn it in for cash a second time.

YOUNG GIRL: Perhaps I ought to get up.

OLD MAN: Oh, it's still early. By the looks of the sun I'd say it's around seven o'clock. At your age you ought to have at least nine hours of sleep. What do you and your group do in the daytime?

YOUNG GIRL: I don't know about the others, but I go back home and help my mother. I go to the movies sometimes.

OLD MAN: You really have a mother? I can't believe it.

YOUNG GIRL: Come on, don't be silly. Don't you have any children?

OLD MAN: I have one daughter. This hurts, coming from you.

YOUNG GIRL: So that's why I feel like a daughter to you.

OLD MAN: No, I'm not thinking of you as my daughter. No, not at all. You are something very, very different, something very special.

YOUNG GIRL: What is that supposed to mean? You mean I am grown up for my age?

OLD MAN: Oh, I wouldn't say that, but you--how should I put it?--I feel so much more comfortable being with you than with my own daughter. I don't have to feel nervous around you.

YOUNG GIRL: Your daughter, is your daughter that dreadful?

OLD MAN: No, I wouldn't say that exactly. But at least I find her hard to handle. I have to always watch how she is going to react to things.

You see you can never tell what she is going to do next. I can't very well look the other way, and the first thing I know I say something. Then she turns and strikes out at me.

YOUNG GIRL: She hits you?

OLD MAN: No. She doesn't actually hit me, but she gives me a tongue lashing, and this is what happens every time. I suppose I have to accept part of the blame for spoiling her. She reacts this way to nobody but her father. It's not often that you find a daughter who relentlessly lashes out at her only surviving parent.

YOUNG GIRL: That's because you are too easy on her--you give in too easily. Why don't you bawl her out? There's nothing to it. But you can't do it, can you?

OLD MAN: I think you're right about my being too easy on her, but I can't change suddenly. Sure, I could easily bawl her out. But then what? How would she take it? Her mother was a high spirited woman and her daughter inherited that trait. To make matters worse, I just don't know how to handle women.

YOUNG GIRL: You are right. You ought to know that women have a predisposition for getting up on their high horse. I'm like that, too, in some ways.

OLD MAN: You may be right, but then I can't tell just by spending one night with you. Well, I have stayed long enough. I'll be running along.

*The Old Man moves from stage right in the direction of stage left.*

OLD MAN: Hey, it's me, your father. Open the door.

DAUGHTER: What have you been doing all this time?

OLD MAN: Come on, you open the door! I'll tell you about it later.

DAUGHTER: I stayed up till one o'clock last night waiting for you. I couldn't go to bed without locking up.

OLD MAN: I know, I know. I walked out because you told me I was a nuisance.

DAUGHTER: That's because you kept blubbering when I was trying to read.

OLD MAN: Blubbering! What needs to be said has to be said.

DAUGHTER: I have had my breakfast.

OLD MAN: I haven't yet.

DAUGHTER: Not really, the soup's all cold.

OLD MAN: I'll have it cold. It must be about time for you to leave.

DAUGHTER: Of course it is. What time do you think it is?

OLD MAN: I don't really care what time it is, but I can tell that it is time for you to leave.

DAUGHTER: Today's our company holiday and we're all going to Kamakura.

OLD MAN: You don't have to sound so angry, do you, when you say that?

DAUGHTER: I cooked some rice this morning but that's for my lunch box. Help yourself to the rice in the other cooker. It hasn't been warmed up.

OLD MAN: I would rather have it cold. There is a lot of it, isn't there?

DAUGHTER: That's to take care of your three meals. There isn't time to prepare any side dishes for your lunch and dinner.

OLD MAN: Oh, don't worry, I'll make out somehow. What are you taking for lunch?

DAUGHTER: Meat preserves and egg rolls.

OLD MAN: Hummmm, sound's pretty good. Don't forget to take some pickled plums.

DAUGHTER: You know very well that I don't like pickled plums.

OLD MAN: You'd better put it in your lunch box anyway as an antiseptic.

DAUGHTER: Oh, don't be so old-fashioned.

OLD MAN: So, you're going to Kamakura. Are you getting better at swimming?

DAUGHTER: Where on earth did you stay last night?

OLD MAN: I'm wondering if I should tell you or not.

DAUGHTER: You don't have to tell me if you don't want to. Couldn't have been a respectable place, anyway.

OLD MAN: I'm amazed at you. You take your father to be that kind of a man?

DAUGHTER: You can never tell about men.

OLD MAN: I don't know who told you things like that, but it's wrong to regard all men in that way, least of all your own father. What a way to talk to an old man like me.

DAUGHTER: Oh, I was just teasing you. You couldn't possibly do things like that.

OLD MAN: And if I could?

DAUGHTER: If you could it would be really funny.

OLD MAN: All right, you are entirely wrong. What do you mean, it would be funny if I could? You make it a habit of ridiculing your father at the first opportunity. The fact that I can't stay at a respectable place, what is so funny about that?

DAUGHTER: Don't take me so seriously. It's like being honest to a fault. Flirting with girls is nothing unusual with men. It's not a case of good or bad. Of course for appearance sake one would have to say it is bad. And that's acceptable to society. I have heard of no one proclaim that he wouldn't flirt with women because he felt that it was not a good thing to do. And there are others who would like to flirt with women, but can't. But this is a rather funny situation.

OLD MAN: You talk as though you knew all about life. But aren't you contradicting yourself? You said just now that it was funny that some people couldn't go through with what they wanted to do. But didn't you tell me a while ago that it would be funny if I could?

DAUGHTER: That's why I say it's even funnier to see somebody who forces himself to do something which he couldn't possibly bring himself to do. You went to see my aunt in Shibuya, didn't you? I know that's where you went.

OLD MAN: No.

DAUGHTER: Where else would you go then? The old gentleman at Sagamiya has long been bedridden.

OLD MAN: You are still wrong.

DAUGHTER: Watch what you're doing. You're spilling rice. Don't step on it again.

OLD MAN: You are a stubborn one. All right, I'll tell you. Your father spent a night at a very good place. You are old enough for me to tell you about it. For the first time in his life, your father had a visit with a gentle girl.

DAUGHTER: Well, listen to him talk. I can't imagine what kind of a girl would keep you company.

OLD MAN: Just what I thought. I know you wouldn't have the slightest idea. Frankly, neither could I.

DAUGHTER: You probably picked up a streetwalker in the dark.

OLD MAN: It was rather dark. I'd hardly call her a streetwalker.

DAUGHTER: How disgusting!

OLD MAN: That's one way of looking at it. But actually there's more than meets the eye. I gave her some money, but all I did was to spend a little while talking with her in a hotel room. I had her go to bed alone and I sat on the sofa and thought about things. And as dawn approached, I dozed off.

DAUGHTER: I'm not interested in hearing anything more. In any case, how could you bring yourself to say such things in front of your own daughter? How old was she, that girl?

OLD MAN: Nineteen.

DAUGHTER: Not really! Father, have you gone out of your mind?

OLD MAN: A little bit perhaps. It's something that I wouldn't ordinarily do. Do you realize that not once in my life have I been spoken to with tenderness by my mother, by my wife, or even by my own daughter? Well, perhaps that is a little biased. But at any rate, from the heart and freely.

DAUGHTER: What kind of a remark is that? You're saying that you can feel more at ease with a streetwalker than you can with your own daughter? What do you mean by that? The very idea, comparing me to a streetwalker!

OLD MAN: One can't make comparison, that's true. And I'm not doing it, either. I'm sorry I didn't say it in the right way.

DAUGHTER: I can't speak for grandmother or mother, but as far as I am concerned, I am the way I am, and if I may say so I feel that I have done all that is expected of a daughter.

OLD MAN: Are you suggesting then that I'm not doing what is expected of me as your father?

DAUGHTER: I don't know. That's not for me to decide. Nobody told me how much a parent is supposed to do for his children, and I never thought about it.

OLD MAN: That's as it should be. I don't particularly care for you to find out or even to think about it. But you say you are doing all that you should be doing as my daughter. Well, you may be right. But I wish you could be a little gentler in your ways. I wish you had a warm concern for me. And even if you didn't mean it, I wish you could express your love as love in your eyes and face.

DAUGHTER: Strangers are bound to be gentler in their attitudes. They have everything to gain by it.

OLD MAN: You have a point there. But does it follow that just because you have nothing actually to gain, you should be so hard on me?

DAUGHTER: Why, I'm not hard on you at all. What a thing to say!

OLD MAN: See, there you go again. Why do you have to speak in such an angry tone. That's a form of a threat, you know. And threats are made because you can gain something by it. It isn't just a question of losing ground. I can only assume that you are hard on me because you hope to gain something by it.

DAUGHTER: Why, I haven't gained a thing!

OLD MAN: Sure, the results are the same. It's like begging for something which one doesn't have. It's just that you get a feeling that you are gaining something.

DAUGHTER: How tiresome! Don't you know that elderly people are sweet when they are quiet?

OLD MAN: There have been times when I have been quiet. But when did you ever tell me I was sweet?

DAUGHTER: The trouble with you, father, is that you're always butting into somebody else's business.  You keep repeating over and over what is perfectly obvious.

OLD MAN: I suppose this is a weakness common to elderly people.

DAUGHTER: You have gone way beyond that. You're a special case.

OLD MAN: What, a special case?

DAUGHTER: An exceptionally bad case.

OLD MAN: Oh, it couldn't be as bad as all that.

DAUGHTER: You don't realize it yourself.  Ask anybody.

OLD MAN: If they think I'm a special case?

DAUGHTER: And besides, you are so ignorant of the new age.  Just because she is a girl doesn't mean that she keeps on saying "yes" to everything her parents say anymore.

OLD MAN: Now, that's something else again.  I have no intention, absolutely no intention of making you say "yes" to everything I say. I'm not suggesting that you practice filial piety.  You're free and don't think your father hasn't been open-minded about this.  All I ask is that you realize that your father is still very much alive and that you do not insult him unnecessarily.

DAUGHTER: I have no intention of insulting you, although I must say that I can't exactly respect you.  Sure, I was taught at school that you should honor your parents, but can I help it if there is nothing in you that I can respect?

OLD MAN: Well, that's true.  I'm not asking you to respect me.

DAUGHTER: In the first place, what is there in you that makes you worthy of respect?  You don't regard yourself as something special, do you?

OLD MAN: You're right.  I don't.

DAUGHTER: You know, that's the one thing I like about you, Father.

OLD MAN: That was a real nice thing you said.

DAUGHTER: And then there's another thing.  You always have a way of getting money from somewhere--I don't know where.  I'm amazed how the money continues.

OLD MAN: I don't know how long it will.

DAUGHTER: It hasn't been too hard on you, has it?

OLD MAN: It isn't easy to deal in antiques without capital.  But still, my eyes are sharper than others and sometimes I come across a real find at a bargain.

DAUGHTER: If only I made twice as much!  We could manage on my salary.

OLD MAN: Say, isn't it time for you to leave?  Are you ready?

DAUGHTER: I have plenty of time. We don't have to be at Tokyo station till nine.

OLD MAN: That's what you always say and then you are late. You shouldn't make others worry.

DAUGHTER: I know, I know. I wonder if I would be too warm in this today. I think I would be more comfortable in a sleeveless one-piece dress. Don't you think so?

OLD MAN: It's a fine time to be thinking about that. If you're going to change, hurry up and change.

DAUGHTER: That's why I'm asking you if you think I would be too warm.

OLD MAN: What do you have to ask me for as long as you aren't too warm.

DAUGHTER: I'm not asking you about that.

OLD MAN: I think you would be better off in a sleeveless one-piece dress.

DAUGHTER: Thank you. I don't look good in a sleeveless one-piece dress.

OLD MAN: Oh, I didn't realize.

DAUGHTER: Ah, What's the point of getting all dolled up? Just look at my lips? What good would lipstick do?

OLD MAN: Let me have a look.

DAUGHTER: Let me see--nothing! They look just like your lips. My lower lip sticks out and I hardly have an upper lip.

OLD MAN: It doesn't look that bad to me.

DAUGHTER. Really, I can't do a thing about this face of mine. It's an amazing face, if I say so myself.

OLD MAN: It's too bad you didn't take after your mother.

DAUGHTER: I don't mean that. It's just that I wish you were somebody else.

OLD MAN: Oh.

DAUGHTER: I know that nobody would want to marry me. I might as well go to a nunnery.

OLD MAN: You always run to extremes. You most certainly are not as unattractive as you think. When I walk along the street I see any number of young women who are no more attractive than you.

DAUGHTER: See, just as I said. There are far more unattractive women in this world than otherwise.

OLD MAN: All I'm saying is that you're as attractive as anybody else. And don't forget I'm being very modest in my appraisal. You see, what makes a woman attractive is not what's on the outside, but what comes from within--a gentleness of character, intelligence, and passion--you know, in the good sense of the term.

DAUGHTER: Thank you, I've heard enough. I hope the girls you give birth to in the future will turn out that way.

OLD MAN: In the future. Don't joke like that. You're just impossible.

DAUGHTER: It could happen, you know.

OLD MAN: But even if you thought so, why do you have to say things like that to my face? Why get so hysterical about it?

DAUGHTER: Hysterical, he says. Ha! How ridiculous.

OLD MAN: I'm the one that feels ridiculous.

DAUGHTER: So both of us feel that way. Isn't that all right?

OLD MAN: I say that and she says this.

DAUGHTER: And I say this and he says that.

OLD MAN: And there's no end to it.

DAUGHTER: Father, don't you honestly feel that I'm a nuisance?

OLD MAN: I will not dignify that with an answer.

DAUGHTER: You act as if the whole thing is just too much of a burden.

OLD MAN: Well, there are times when I can't help feeling like that.

DAUGHTER: What would you do if I left home?

OLD MAN: Don't torture me like that, please.

DAUGHTER: I'm not torturing you. I just want to know, that's all.

OLD MAN: That is precisely what I mean by torture. What's the matter with you?

DAUGHTER: You know, Father, I feel I have really found out today what you are really like.

OLD MAN: That goes for me, too. For the first time today, I think I know what you are really like.

DAUGHTER: You're disappointed, aren't you?

OLD MAN: How about you?

DAUGHTER: The same. It hasn't changed anything, for better or worse.

OLD MAN: I feel the same way, too. Except that I realize that perhaps I have been a wee bit narrow-minded.

DAUGHTER: I've also realized something; that I was perhaps taking you, Father, too much for granted. I had forgotten the fact that you are, after all, a man. I'm sorry.

OLD MAN: You don't have to apologize. I feel embarrassed to have you apologize to me. You can go on snapping at me as you have. Now I feel more confident about being able to sense your love for me in between those snaps. You'd better hurry, you'll be late.

DAUGHTER: I'm on my way, then. If anybody should come while I'm gone, don't get involved in a long and worthless conversation as you did the other day.

OLD MAN: I have never done a thing like that, have I?

DAUGHTER: What a short memory you have. Remember the fellow who was fired from the store Shiroki? I hear he came to see me last Sunday and then you had to tell him that I was at the Subaru theatre. He followed me there and I just didn't know what to do with him.

OLD MAN: But he seemed to have a general idea of your plans.

DAUGHTER: But even so, you didn't have to fall for it, did you? It is so embarrassing.

OLD MAN: I'll be more careful.

DAUGHTER: The trouble with you is that it isn't going to do any good. You are sort of senile.

OLD MAN: I'll see what I can do about that, too. When do you expect to be back?

DAUGHTER: I don't know. I'll get back when I want to.

OLD MAN: Thank you. Watch out for those summer waves down at Yuigahama Beach. After all, I have to have my say, too.

*Curtain.*

## SOURCES

The Japanese texts of the plays in this collection are available in the following sources:

*Paper Balloon* (*Kami fûsen*) is included in *Gendai nihon bungaku zenshû*, vol. 33 (Chikuma shobô, 1955), pp. 287-292.

*Autumn in the Tyrols* (*Chiroru no aki*): *Gendai nihon gikyoku senshû*, vol. 6 (Hakusuisha, 1955), pp. 381-395.

*Cloudburst* (*Shûu*) may be found in *Kishida Kunio zenshû*, vol. 1 (Shinchôsha, 1954), pp. 141-158.

The text of *A Diary of Fallen Leaves* (*Ochiba nikki*) is also available in *Kishida Kunio zenshû*, vol. 1, pp. 286-313.

The translation of *The Two Daughters of Mr. Sawa* (*Sawa-shi no futari musume*) is based on the text in *Gendai nihon gikyoku senshû*, vol. 6 (Hakusuisha, 1955), pp. 343-379.

*Adoration* (*Nyonin katsugô*) is included in *Gendai nihon bungaku zenshû*, vol. 33, pp. 374-383.

# CORNELL EAST ASIA SERIES

FORTHCOMING

*The Gods Come Dancing: A Study of the Japanese Ritual Dance of
Yamabushi Kagura*, by Irit Averbuch

*Restless Spirits: Fourth Category Japanese Noh Plays*, Parallel Translations with Running Commentary, by Chifumi Shimazaki

*Singing Like a Cricket, Hooting Like an Owl: Selected Poems by Yi Kyu-
bo*, translated by Kevin O'Rourke

*Back to Heaven: Selected Poems of Ch'ŏn Sang Pyŏng*, translated by
Brother Anthony of Taizé and Young-Moo Kim

*Korean Adoption and Inheritance: Case Studies in the Creation of a
Classic Confucian Society*, by Mark Peterson

For ordering information, please contact the Cornell East Asia Series,
East Asia Program, Cornell University, 140 Uris Hall, Ithaca, NY
14853-7601, USA; phone (607) 255-6222, fax (607) 255-1388.

4-95/.6M/TS